Guy'd Lines

Rules for Living
From My 30 Years as a Psychotherapist

When the pain of change becomes less then the pain of
remaining the same,
And the fear of change becomes less then the fear of
remaining the same,
Then the anxiety of change becomes excitement.

With the realization that change is inevitable,
"Good and bad times become one" : Learning
Growth becomes the quest,
Living in the moment is the process and love of life is
the answer.

Please visit **www.guydlinesforyou.com**
or **www.crossroads73.com** for more information.
Thank you.

Guy'd Lines

Rules for Living
From My 30 Years as a Psychotherapist

By
Guy W. Shilts, Jr., MS, LMFT, LPC, LCSW

Crossroads Psychological Services
Janesville, Wisconsin

Guy'd Lines
Rules for Living
From My 30 Years
As a Psychotherapist

1st Edition

Crossroads Psychological Services, LLC
For information address:
17 South River Street
P.O. 858
Janesville, WI 53547
www.crossroads73.com

This book is intended for educational purposes, and the information presented is not a substitute for psychotherapy.

Printed in the United States of America

ISBN: 0-9778542-0-5

This book is dedicated to my teachers:
My family
My friends
My patients

Acknowledgements

I want to thank my wife Bev for her quiet, steadfast support since 1967, for allowing me to be myself, for her creativity and for her uncanny ability to make complex ideas simple. I'd also like to thank Sue Schroeder for providing the impetus for this book, for coining the word "Guyisms" and for encouraging me to write a book. A big thank you also goes to Jim Tullis, Tim Perry and Barb Knapton for their support and loyalty, to my siblings Mary, Nancy and Doug for their courage to face our family's truths and their willingness to work together, to Don "Butch" Vogt, Katherine Weidner and Kathy Helgeson for their roles as patient consultants, to Gary Gandy for his wonderful illustrations, to Mary Jo Fahey for her technical expertise, to Lisa Wilber for her graphic design, and to Sharon Vanorny for her photography. I'd also like to thank my son Will, who taught me about strength and courage, to my son Jordan for his brilliance and his quiet loving ways and to my daughter Megan, who is one of the strongest and most tenacious people I've ever met.

About the Author

Guy Shilts, Jr.

All of my life experiences have contributed to my work as a therapist. They've enhanced my formal education, intuition, worldview, and spirituality, and they've also given me clues about how to conquer my personal challenges. All of the people I have met have also helped me become a better therapist—including my wife and children. The work of a psychotherapist is unlike that of other professions. Surgeons, CPAs, architects and others can create a life compartment for their career and keep it separate from their personal life. In contrast, a psychotherapist needs to draw on every life experience and totally integrate every lesson throughout life. I've tried to include many of the lessons I learned that helped shape who I am as a therapist. I hope that my story will not only help you learn about me, but also about the people who helped me along the way.

Polio At Age Five

Although I grew up in a conservative Midwestern home, I've always been an unpredictable rebel who was naturally drawn to counseling. On April 29, 1947, my mother was in labor for 28 hours in Chicago's Ravenswood Hospital. She had pre-eclampsia, high blood pressure and double-vision. The doctors thought they could save her, but I wasn't expected to survive. I guess I was determined even then. At five, I was stricken with polio and spent two months in a hospital crib. For two long weeks I was totally paralyzed from the neck down. All of my limbs recovered except for my left arm and shoulder.

My Visits With the Children at Wesley Memorial Hospital

Even as a little kid I was able to relate to other people and their situations. While I was hospitalized with polio I was

Quote: "Here is the test to find whether your mission on Earth is finished: if you're alive, it isn't."

      - Richard Bach
        Author
        *Jonathan
        Livingston
        Seagull*

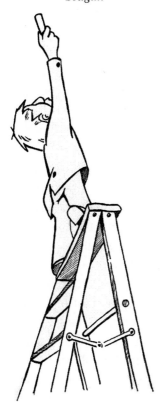

able to move around the floor to talk to the older children and cheer them up. Many of the teenagers had to be placed in iron lungs and it was very painful to see all the suffering in that ward. I'll never forget the young woman in the next room who had a baby while she was in an iron lung. There was a lot of crying in her room and I told my mom that God was there that day and He was crying too.

I wanted so badly to help the other kids and one day I came up with a plan to help the little girl in the crib next to mine. I thought if I could get her out of her crib (or cage, as I used to think of it) then we could play together. I crawled into her crib, but was unable to pull her up —she was paralyzed from the waist down. Since my legs had recovered by this point I spent much of my time making rounds with my mother, who had taken a job as an RN at the hospital, visiting anyone who wanted to talk. I was one of only two children who recovered enough to be able to walk out of the hospital.

Schizophrenia and Alcoholism in My Family

I also saw a lot of psychological illness before the age of ten. My schizophrenic grandmother helped raise me. She had a lot of fear, and I had to reassure her more than once that there was no such thing as a machine that controlled people's thoughts. At times, it seems like I had to take care of her more than she had to take care of me. Her husband (Boppa) was my hero. He was a downstate Illinois farm boy who made it big. As a young man he took a job as an office boy at Johnson Controls and worked his way up to become the Assistant Treasurer, yet he remained a very humble and kind man. He and Nana both had a huge influence on my life. On my mother's side, we had severe alcoholism with her brother Jimmy and her stepfather Roy. Before I had my driver's license, Roy used to take me to bars with him so I could drive him home. Luckily, that didn't happen often because by that time I had moved to Wisconsin and didn't see him very much.

Learning About Counseling As a Career

I never liked school until I got to college. I am dyslexic (probably because I had to switch from left-handedness to right after I had polio) and had trouble reading. I had a great auditory memory that helped me get through the lower grades. An eighth grade teacher told my parents I was retarded, so I was put on a slower track. All my school years were kind of an uphill battle, but this was probably the lowest point! Later on I took the Stanford Benet IQ test, and scored much higher than average, so I set my sights on college where I was encouraged by my parents to get a business degree. Although I probably did more drinking than studying, I managed to earn my BBA in four and a half years. I went right on to graduate school in business, but I wasn't very happy and felt out of sync with my fellow business students. I started seeing a college counselor and it was during one of my sessions that I realized I wanted to make a career change. I said to my therapist, "I'd be great at what you do." She agreed, and two weeks later I transferred to the college's new counseling department and got a graduate assistantship with one of the professors. I had found my calling. I got my Masters in Counseling in less than 1 1/2 years, graduating in the midst of the country's recession in the early seventies.

Quote: "I have always grown from my problems and challenges, from the things that don't work out, that's when I've really learned."

- Carol Burnett
Comedian

Founding Crossroads In the Midst of a Recession

When I left school I couldn't find a job, so I spent time volunteering at the college's counseling center. The rebel in me came to the rescue—I decided if no one wanted to hire me, I'd just start something myself! I joined up with one of the professors from school, Dick Wagner, and my wife's best friend's husband, Bob Long, and we opened up a small counseling center. We had visions of doing this for about five years and then moving on. Dick and Bob both did move on, but here I am 30+ years later, doing business just a few blocks from where we started. Crossroads Counseling Center has grown from three people providing 250 hours of therapy per year to 40 people providing 32,000 hours of therapy each year.

My Wife and Children Have Taught Me a Lot

I met my wife, Bev, in college and we've been together for more than thirty years. We were married in 1970 and we have three wonderful children. My family has taught me more about love, life, triumph and tragedy than I could ever have imagined. The trials, tribulations and joys that we have experienced together have had a profound effect on my ability to help other people, and I am eternally grateful for all that I have learned.

I Certainly Don't Have All The Answers

My point in telling you that I have experienced both triumphs and tragedies is so that you understand that I certainly don't have all the answers and I am not immune to difficulties that life presents. I will experience pain and joy in my life just as you will. But if I can help you navi-

Quote: "Our most basic common link is that we all inhabit this planet. We all breathe the same air. We all cherish our children's future. And we are all mortal."

- John F. Kennedy

gate through some of the psychological land mines that are out there, I think I've done my job.

Facing Your Own Truths As You Learn to Make Choices

This book is an introduction to many of the recurring themes that I learned from observing my patients in the past thirty years. As in life, psychotherapy is a process of discovery—of yourself, your environment and the relationships around you. Readers will discover that many of the themes overlap. This seems to agree with the fact that psychotherapeutic growth, for all of us, is a blending of art, science and spirituality. Most of all, the growth that we all experience deals with facing our truths as we learn to make choices, not from a fear-based position but from a healthy, love-based position.

About This Book

Readers will soon discover my Guyisms, or expressions that I call Rules. They're sayings that I've invented over the years as I've learned about human behavior, and they form the basis of each chapter. I started this project with a list of of 40 or 50 rules and I picked a baker's dozen of my favorites for this book.

Patient Stories and Self-Help Exercises

The patient stories in this book have been added to help illustrate the ideas in each chapter. In most cases, names and situational facts have been changed to protect each person's privacy. Occasionally, you'll find stories about patients who asked that their real names be used. By themselves, patient stories are instructive but each chapter also needed self-help exercises and step-by-step intructions that resemble the tools I use in person. Some authors in the field of self-development create books and then publish a separate workbook. This book provides conceptual information and self-help exercises in an all-in-one format.

Quotes, Tips and FYIs

I've used the wide margins on each page to hold extras in the form of quotes, tips and fyis. Some of the extras are related to the content in each of the chapters, but most are designed to provide a little relief from the subject of family dysfunction. Many of the quotes are humorous and I hope they will provide a little levity when you read about dysfunction and realize that you have some crazy patterns in your life that you didn't know about.

Quote: "Laughter and tears are both responses to frustration and exhaustion. I myself prefer to laugh, since there is less cleaning up to do afterward."

- Kurt Vonnegut
  Author

The Cartoons and the Cartoonerators

The cartoons were created last and they were fun to produce. I had a team that helped and I call them the "cartoonerators." First came the captions and then the illustrations—straight out of artist Gary Gandy's imagination. Gary has been drawing caricatures at Crossroads for a long time. He's drawn very funny murals on our walls and I'm delighted that his artwork is now part of this book. The cartoon figures you see on this page and the next are just a few of the drawings that you'll see scattered throughout the chapters.

"By shedding a new light on the ghosts of the past, my patients can look towards a brighter future."

More About Gary

Gary's work can best be described as "diversified." Not only is he an accomplished cartoon illustrator, but he has also delved into nature, wildlife and urban realism painting. He has over thirty published limited edition prints, a dozen poster images and numerous logo designs and illustrations. Gary is both a concept artist and an application artist, not only designing his ideas but also building them through his interior design business. He has also created many murals for his interior design projects.

In 1994, Gary was the only artist allowed to paint a historic portrait of the white buffalo calf born in southern Wisconsin. The painting was exhibited by the United States Department of the Interior for 26 months.

Gary feels it's his sense of humor and his vast library of self-help books that have helped him survive what he calls a "nearly impossible business." As he explains, "I return to the things that make me laugh. Bringing a cartoon character to life right before your eyes can erase all the difficulties life throws at you. And, ironically, unlike all my other forms of expression, they seem to come to life all by themselves." Gary can be contacted at garymgandy@ sbcglobal.net.

Notes

Table of Contents

Chapter 2 91

Rule #2: The Things People Say to Themselves—I Would Not Say to My Worst Enemy

Chapter 3 127

Rule #3: When You Consistently Under or Over-React Emotionally to People, Places or Things, It's Probably Transference

Chapter 5

Rule #5: We Do Not Change Our Core Personality— We Just Learn to Work With It

Chapter 12 327

Rule #12: The Best Predictor of Future Behavior Is Past Behavior Unless the Person Works Very Hard to Change

Chapter 13 337

Rule #13: Don't Take It Personally, It's Just Their Personality (Disorder)—They Do This to Everyone

Notes

INTRODUCTION

It Would Be Great to Start Life At 20 Knowing What I Know at Fifty-Nine

Forewarned, forearmed; to be prepared is half the victory.

- Miguel de Cervantes
  Author, *Don Quixote de la Mancha*

"When I was 23, while enrolled in a counseling practicum, the professor who was evaulating me at the time said, "Guy, you're going to be a really good therapist some day—all you need is gray hair." My youthful arrogance prevented me from understanding what he meant. Many years later, I understand that it takes time to be a good therapist. Wisdom comes with a price."

Guyisms Are Observations About Human Nature

When I decided to write a book about my thirty years in psychotherapy, I wanted to create a handbook for twenty-somethings who were just starting their lives. I thought about how great it would be to start life at twenty knowing what I know at fifty-nine.

For the past ten years, my colleagues at Crossroads Counseling have goaded me about recording my "Guyisms" in a book. I call them rules, as in "rules of thumb." Some rules are strict principles that are considered to be regulations. Mine are simply observations about human nature based on my experience as a psychotherapist. I consider them to be clues to the complex puzzle we call life.

Most of the work that I do within the field of psychotherapy is called talk therapy. I've counseled dozens of patients each week for over thirty years and when I began to notice patterns of behavior, I knew the patterns could be used as tools to help a lot of other people.

Most of this book is about the truths that we've inherited from our families. People spend a lifetime obeying the rules created by other people and the result is that they become someone who they are not. Even when people deliberately choose therapy and know that they want to change, their beliefs are usually so strong that they have never stopped to consider their heart's desire.

Life Is About Choices

If there's an area of your life that you would like to change, use the rules as guides or suggestions while you're working on your changes. It's important to understand that everyone has absolute choices concerning the truth that they create in their life. Many books have been

Quote: "The human mind is our fundamental resource."

– John F. Kennedy

written about the connection between our thoughts and our reality. As you read each chapter, remember that anything we give our attention to becomes our personal truth. Our repetitive thoughts become our beliefs and life has a way of delivering experiences that match our beliefs.

Something Big Is About to Happen in Your Life

Once someone makes a decision to change, something big starts to happen:

• Decisions are related to choices

• Choices are related to what we desire

• Desires are related to feelings

• Positive and negative feelings help us attract positive and negative changes (See: Learn About Valence to Get What You Want).

Client-Centered Therapy

As a therapist, I know that I have very much been influenced by psychologist Carl Rogers, who used the expression *organismic valuing* to refer to a person's ability to decide what is good for them. In his view, successful therapy occurs when a patient begins doing what they *want* to do and not what they think they should do or what other people think they should do. He also referred to vast resources that each person has within himself for:

• self-understanding

• altering self-concept, attitudes and behavior

Quote: "One of the frailties of the human condition—people fear that which is not familiar."

- Spike Lee
Filmmaker

Rogers developed his theory over fifty years ago and it's interesting to see Rogerian themes in modern self-development work that emphasizes autonomy and freedom with responsibility.

Tapping Into the Power of Intention

Dr. Wayne Dyer, who has written twenty-five books on the subject of self-development, often speaks about harnessing an innate power inside of ourselves and doing what we *want* to do.

Patients come to therapy because they feel helpless and unable to make decisions or direct their lives. Facilitating an environment that provides patients with an ability to throw off anything that prevents them from realizing their potential is very much the Rogerian approach to self-empowerment.

In his latest book, titled *The Power of Intention*, Dyer speaks about an evolution in his career that came about when he read two sentences in Carlos Castaneda's final book, *The Active Side of Infinity*:

> "Intent is a force that exists in the universe. When sorcerers (those who live of the Source[1]) beckon intent, it comes to them and sets up a path for attainment, which means that sorcerers always accomplish what they set out to do."

[1] Source refers to God.

Many years ago, I watched Oprah Winfrey talk with Tina Turner when she was a guest on Oprah's show. As they spoke about Tina's success at surmounting the challenges

Quote: "Every human being is the author of his own health or disease."

- Buddha

in her life, they both mentioned the power of intention. At the time, I assumed that they were referring to Tina's strong will. I now realize that they may have been referring to the intention-as-a-force in the universe that Wayne Dyer described in his book. He says, "Intention is a power that's present everywhere as a field of energy […] As you make your metaphorical bow to this power, recognize that you are bowing to yourself. The all-pervading energy of intention pulses toward your intention for a purposeful life."

In *The Four Agreements*, author Don Miguel Ruiz says that our intent manifests through our word. He writes:

"Your word is the power that you have to create. Our word is the gift that comes directly from God. The Gospel of John in the Bible, speaking of the creation of the universe, says, 'In the beginning was the word, and the word was with God, and the word is God.' Through your word you express your creative power. It is through the word that you manifest everything. Regardless of what language you speak, your intent manifests through the word."

Tap the Energy of Intention as You Read the Rules

Chapter 2 is about the power of positive self-talk but it is really an important theme that affects every chapter. As you're reading each chapter, if you feel that the ideas relate to you, use the power of spoken intentions. Here are some suggestions to say aloud:

Chapter	Topic	Intention to Say Aloud (or invent your own)
1	Roles	"I intend to choose more effective roles in my new life."
2	Self-Talk	"I intend to say positive things to myself."
3	Transference	"I intend to notice my emotional triggers and understand them."
4	Codependency	"I intend to take care of myself and advocate for my own needs."
5	Personality Types	"I intend to learn my loved one's personality types and understand their needs."
6	Marriage	"I intend to be a good team member."
7	Communication Tools	"I intend to learn great communication techniques."
8	Control	"I intend to cooperate through mutual benefit."
9	Perceptions	"I intend to step out of the box and invent a new life."
10	Intuition	"I intend to listen to my gut."
11	Denial	"I intend to always break through my toxic denial."
12	Predictive Behavior	"I intend to be patient and understand how past behavior is a prediction of future behavior."
13	Personality Disorders	"I intend to detach from my personality-disordered loved one."

Preparing for Your Purposeful Life

Previously, when I said that something "Big" is about to happen, I was referring to your decision to make changes in your life. The journey is important and so is your preparation. Here are some important elements.

Work at Being Creative

If you're about to re-invent your life, you will need to work at being creative and stimulate your imagination. Mihaly Csikszentmihalyi, who wrote *Creativity: Flow and the Psychology of Discovery and Invention*, says, "A creative accomplishment is almost never the result of a sudden insight, a light bulb flashing on in the dark, but comes after years of hard work." He names four main conditions that are important during the creative process. Even though his book is about inventors and scientists, it is easy to see that these conditions are equally as important for anyone who is reinventing their life:

- Pay Attention to the Developing Work and Notice when New Ideas, New Problems and New Insights Arise

- Pay Attention to One's Goals and Feelings

- Keep in Touch with The Most Effective Techniques

- Listen to Colleagues

It is interesting to note that Csikszentmihalyi says creative work is never done. His chapter on enhancing personal creativity contains advice for cultivating creative flow in everyday life. He says we can learn to use creative energy so that it generates its own internal force to keep us focused, avoid depression and increase our capacity to relate to the world.

Tip: Numerous books instruct readers on how to think creatively, including:

The Creative Habit: Learn It and Use It for Life by Twyla Tharp

A Whack on the Side of the Head: How You Can Be More Creative by von Oech

Handbook of Creativity by Robert J. Sternberg

Thinkertoys: A Handbook of Creative Thinking Techniques by Michael Michalko

Wake Up With a Specific Goal to Look Forward To

Csikszentmihalyi says creative people are eager to start the day. They believe there is something meaningful to accomplish and they can't wait to get started on it. He says it does not matter if at first our goals are trivial and not interesting. The important thing is to take easy first steps.

Note: Even if you don't feel creative—pretend that you are! Psych yourself up because the job of re-inventing your life requires attention and work.

If You Do Anything Well, It Becomes Enjoyable

According to Csikszentmihalyi, we can practice improving the quality of everyday activities and then tackle something more difficult.

Note: Pretend that the job of re-inventing your life is a course and you're going to do whatever it takes to get an A. If I can squeeze thirty years of psychotherapy into a book for you to read, you can go over it and over it until you learn every word! Realize that no one changes overnight. Don't give up!

To Continue to Enjoy Something, You Need to Increase Its Complexity

Csikszentmihalyi explains that in order to enjoy the same activity over and over, you will need to discover new challenges and new opportunities in it. He says it is always possible to find a better way to do anything. That is why creativity—the attempts to expand our boundaries—makes a lifetime of enjoyment possible.

Note: To expand your boundaries, consider digging deeper into each of the topics I've presented. I've added many references to the text and margins of this book for

Quote: "Even if I knew that tomorrow the world would go to pieces, I would still plant my apple tree."

- Martin Luther King, Jr.

readers who want to learn more. As Csikszentmihalyi says, "Creative work is never done."

Scale to Get in Touch With Your Feelings

Chapter 7 introduces the concept of Scaling—a tool that I use to help patients get in touch with their feelings. The chapter introduces the four most basic feelings: mad, sad, glad, afraid.

Although feelings are the key to understanding what we truly desire, many people are surprised to learn that they're not in touch with these most basic feelings. As young children, we're taught what feelings are acceptable, and by the time we're adults we're trained to do what others want us to do. We're taught mostly to please—Mom and Dad, teachers and often our priest or minister. To feel accepted, we agree to other people's thoughts and feelings.

The Scaling tool in this book is provocative. It's designed to make people think about how they feel. No one will be able to truly understand what it is that they desire until they get in touch with their own feelings. Life is about making choices, and life's experiences can be described as things that we want or don't want. If any of the circumstances in your life are causing you pain, then they're most likely "don't wants." You are the only one who is equipped to make choices about what it is that you would like to experience.

Once you learn how to scale, use the technique as your personal geiger counter to zero in on how you feel about your choices:

Quote: "A wonderful fact to reflect upon, that every human creature is constituted to be that profound secret and mystery to every other."

- Charles Dickens

- choices about your work

- choices about your relationships

- choices about where you'd like to live

- choices about how you spend your time

- choices about your education

- choices about your personal projects

No one in your life can tell you what you want. You're the only one who is equipped to make real choices about your life and it's the choices that are related to your heart's desire. In order to understand what you desire, you'll need to register a feeling on your personal geiger counter. If it's a "glad" then you'll know it's for you.

Learn About Valence to Get What You Want

Valence is a concept that I've introduced in Chapter 3, but it's another concept that really affects every chapter in the book. I use the term to describe the strength of emotions or feelings.

You may remember the word valence from science class. In chemistry, atoms are assigned positive or negative numbers to describe their strength in chemical reactions. If you never took chemistry in school—don't worry. All you need to know is that feelings are not all the same. Here are some concepts about valence that also relate to feelings:

- There are strong (and weak) positive feelings.

- There are strong (and weak) negative feelings.

Tip: In their book, *Ask and It is Given,* authors Esther and Jerry Hicks have assembled 22 techniques you can use to strengthen your positive feelings.

• A strong positive feeling can overpower a weaker negative feeling.

• A strong negative feeling can overpower a weaker positive feeling.

• Feelings with the same type of charge will have an additive effect. In other words, two negative feelings will add up to a stronger negative and two positives will add up to a stronger positive.

Of the four basic emotions that you will learn how to scale (Mad, Glad, Sad, Afraid), the only one that is positive is Glad. If you are feeling strong negatives about any of your choices, you may be overpowering or cancelling out your positive feelings.

In order to solve a problem, it's necessary to understand it. As a therapist, my real job is to help patients nurture their positive feelings about themselves. Each time we meet, we examine feelings and reshape many negatives into positives. I can't meet with my readers in person, but I can coach you to:

• get in touch with your feelings (with the scaling tool)

• nurture the positives until they overpower any negatives

There are techniques that you can use to support or strengthen your positive feelings so that they will become strong positives. Positive self-talk is an example, but most of the others are beyond the scope of this book. When topics fall outside the scope of the book, I have placed information in the margins for readers to explore on their own.

Quote: "We are what we repeatedly do. Excellence, then, is not an act, but a habit."

- Aristotle

A Note About Negative Feelings...

Some negative feelings are useful and there are times when we can use negatives (Mad, Sad and Afraid) to make decisions. For example, fear is useful if we're in a dangerous situation. The goal is not to erase our negative feelings, but to:

• understand them

• assess how realistic they are

• create a healthy balance so that they do not obstruct our growth

This Book's Mini-Circuit on Emotions

There's an important mini-circuit in this book on emotions that's worth re-reading once you have finished reading through all the rules. It includes the following topics:

• Intention (stating your intentions aloud)

• Scaling (getting in touch with your feelings)

• Valence (determining the strength of your feelings)

These topics are all related and they're very important. The information in the chapters provides detail, but the book's introduction explains how the topics fit together (in order to get an "A" in this course, you'll need to do some rereading!).

Chapter 1

RULE #1

What Saves Your Ass as a Child Can Hang Your Ass as an Adult

As adults, we usually continue our childhood roles
in the context of a personal relationship

"After working in psychotherapy for a few years, I realized that many of the adults I met were stuck in the roles they had used to navigate their crazy family systems, and that getting "unstuck" meant they needed to learn new roles. In this chapter, we'll explore how to get in touch with the role(s) you may have played as a child, how to determine if you're stuck and how to get unstuck if your childhood role(s) are causing you pain."

Discovering Your Role in a Family System

Note:
As I look back at the adults I've met who came from dysfunctional families, I realize how remarkably strong they were as children.

Wedding vows contain phrases that couples speak in the presence of their friends and families. Along with the traditional pledge that has been spoken for centuries, there's an addition that would be appropriate before the couple is pronounced husband and wife:

> I [name], take thee, [name] to be my wedded partner, to have and to hold from this day forward, to love, honor and cherish, and to live out all my brutal childhood experiences and the defensive roles that saved me—as long as we both shall live.

As children, we take on roles—particularly in households where there is family dysfunction. Roles are used as a defense strategy to survive the traumas of youth, and it's the role that people subconsciously adopt that saves them. Outside the family system, these childhood lifesaving roles work only in appropriate situations. It's the people who don't learn to shape-shift[1] in the world outside the family who get hung. Or, as we say, "What saves their ass, hangs their ass." Later in the book, as we look at the details of how we get hung up, we'll learn about the process of transference, or the unrealistic assigning of emotions experienced in our youth. Our adult lives are full of transference issues that take center stage in relationships with our partners.

---

[1]Shape-shift – an ability to change shape or morph. Shape-shifting has been popularized in science fiction stories such as *The Terminator* and *Star Trek: Deep Space 9*. In this context, we use it to describe the process of transforming roles as you move through life's situations.

Tip: Books are a great help to my clients. For example, Virginia Satir is considered to be the grandmother of family therapy. Her books include: *New Peoplemaking* and *Satir Step by Step: A Guide to Creating Change in Families.*

Statement: "Now that Johnny has gone to the treatment center, we need to pull together."

Translation: "Mom and Dad need another problem child to fix so that they don't have to look at themselves."

Roles exist to maintain a balance in a family system and to make any abnormal behavior appear normal on the surface. Members are usually not conscious of the roles they play. Sometimes, family members exchange roles or play more than one.

The more trouble that exists in a household, the more the members take on rigid roles. In such a group, each family member struggles emotionally to achieve a balance and mask the problem.

The Word *Dysfunction*

Although the word dysfunction is a popular term, it's really not very accurate. In truth, all families function as they work toward equilibrium. Those families that could be called dysfunctional do function but with much more pain. Underneath their pain, they are hiding the truth. For lack of a better term, I'll continue to use the phrase "dysfunctional family."

Family Lie	Truth
Dad has the flu	He's an alcoholic
Dad has a friend	He's having an affair

Family Roles

What are the roles that people play in childhood? Does every family member play a role? Does anyone switch roles or play more than one?

Principal Dysfunctional Member
Some form of an addiction such as substance abuse or compulsive behavior usually marks this role. Because dysfunction is often a multigenerational problem, a principal dysfunctional family member is usually a survivor of early traumas.

Enabler
An enabler is usually a spouse who tries to balance the behavior of the principal dysfunctional member through control. On the surface, it appears that the enabler is the one who is being controlled, but in truth, they have tremendous power. They control passively. If both parents are dysfunctional, they may both be enablers. The out-of-control behavior usually results in abandonment:

Tip: In 1977, Virginia Satir founded AVANTA as a forum for the continual evolution of Satir theory and practice. Headquartered in Burien, Washington, AVANTA has members in 20 countries on five continents.

> AVANTA
> The Virginia Satir
> Network
> 2104 SW 152nd St. #2
> Burien, WA 98166
> (206)241-7566
> www.avanta.net

- Parents abandon children
- Children abandon their childhood
- Spouses abandon each other
- Common sense and reason are abandoned to justify behavior

Hero

The hero child tries to make the family look good. He/she will get straight As in school, excel at sports and assume parent responsibility in the home by taking care of others. Hero children feel they cannot fail and they are usually productive adults.

Tip: *Love Is A Choice: Breaking The Cycle Of Addictive Relationships* by Robert Hemfelt, et. al. is one of my favorite books on codependency.

Rebel

The family rebel is usually blamed for the family pain and making the family look bad. He/she has negative behavior patterns and may wreck the car, get pregnant, get someone else pregnant, abuse drugs, steal or get into fights. Rebels create stress in the family system in an attempt to get the parents to take action. Often, it's the stress and related blame that brings them into counseling. In a stressed family system that's resistant to change, there's plenty of blame. Blame is a form of denial and it's a symptom in a family system whose members do not want to look at themselves.

- The enabler blames the rebel
- The hero blames the rebel
- The rebel blames everyone in the system

Clown

The clown uses humor to relieve tension when the family pain becomes intense.

Lost Child

The lost child tries to escape pain by disappearing into his/her bedroom or some other part of the house. He/she may become overly absorbed in a hobby to run away from pain and is often the silent, "out of reach" family member. Their silence and withdrawal is due to the fact that they do not want to rock the boat.

Tip: Melody Beattie's *Codependent No More: How to Stop Controlling Others and Start Caring for Yourself* has become a classic book on code-pendency.

The roles in a family system sometimes shift from one family member to another. For example, a hero or lost child may take on the role of the rebel when a rebel moves out. In such cases, the family system needs a rebel and a new person takes over the role.

Parenting: Pit Bulls and Wimps

Note:
Out-of-control family situations are usually caused by structural problems—either too much structure or too little.

The parenting styles that are the least effective are the authoritarian pit bulls and the permissive wimps. Rigid, inflexible systems are a breeding ground for unhealthy parent-child relationships and so are loose, chaotic, and self-abandoning environments.

Out-of-Control Families

Although it's possible for mature adults to have a tempermental child with behavior problems, out-of-control families are usually caused by structural problems—either too much structure or too little.

Adults In the Dark

Too often, adult children from these too much or too little families become adults-in-the-dark who have fuzzy ideas about healthy behavior. Here are some examples:

Adult In the Dark	Problem/Solution	Note:
Martha, age forty, has had three marriages. All three of her husbands have complained that she's aloof and does not know how to communicate.	Martha grew up in a household where children were to be "seen and not heard." They rarely provided eye-contact or physical affection and neither parent ever made time for one-on-one activities with any of their children.	Martha needs to learn to incorporate new communication skills into her life. Scientists now know that a person's experiences as a young child and as an adolescent imprint brain pathways that help them form behavioral responses as adults. With practice and

Adult In the Dark	Problem/Solution	Note:
		cooperation from a partner who is able to ask for what he/she needs, a person can adapt and change.
Hugh, whose parents were strict authoritarians, has gone to the opposite extreme to raise his own children, but his laissez-faire parenting style has backfired. His children are unruly and his homelife is hell.	Hugh remembers the pain of feeling disempowered in his youth but now confuses loving behavior with permissiveness.	Unless adults create boundaries or structure, all children will begin to act on impulse and emotion. Hugh needs to learn that loving parents need to create boundaries.
Sharon, who grew up in a home with no rules, no schedules and no guidance from the adults in her life, feels that her life is total chaos and is frequently depressed.	Sharon's adult behavior patterns were influenced by the day-to-day habits that were formed in her youth.	Most adult behavior patterns are firmly fixed in their youth but are not impossible to change if the person works on substituting new behavior patterns for old ones. If the person has been irreparably damaged from parental neglect, habits may be impossible to change.

Learning What's Normal

Note:
If your parents continuously tell you that you are worthless, their insult becomes ingrained in your mind.

Children have little or no frame of reference outside the family. Your relationship with your parents is critical to your emotional stability and mental health. It's often difficult for adults to figure out whether they were abused as children. Let's compare abnormal behavior to behavior that's more normal:

Abnormal	Normal
Parents control their children too much or too little. Patterns of dysfunction emerge at both ends of this continuum.	Children are gently encouraged to be age-appropriately independent (e.g., a two year-old should not be sent to the store by himself/herself).
Parents offer too much approval or too little.	Parents encourage positive self-esteem and realistic self-evaluation.
Family does not socialize; family members are isolated.	Family interacts with a variety of people.
Children fear their parents.	Children are comfortable with both parents.
Child may be given the role of a parent and may be expected to take care of siblings.	Parents function as nurturers.
Parents choose children's activities.	Children are encouraged to pursue their own special interests.

Meet Marilyn

Women are often trained by their mothers to help the boys in the family. Marilyn, who came to see me at age 32, is an example. She had recently found her husband drunk and in bed with another woman. Although she had kicked her husband out of the house, she felt she needed to seek therapy because she wanted her marriage to work.

I asked Marilyn about her childhood.

> "My father was a drunk and now I'm married to one. My father was never able to keep a job and he died at age 50. My mother worked to support three children. It was my job to take care of my two younger brothers. I've always taken care of people. I take care of people everywhere I go—at work and at home. I can't do it anymore."

Marilyn is a classic example of a codependent hero woman who is married to a rebel. The hero and the rebel are both childhood roles that are very common in homes where there is emotional trauma. Codependency, which is described in detail in Chapter 4, is characterized by a loss of personal identity and self-worth.

The hero child grows up thinking that they can help others who are in trouble. In return, they get the limited attention they did as children—from a self-centered partner. Self-worth must be developed from within and the hero child who is unaware of his/her identity is also out of touch with feelings, needs and desires. Through her tears, Marilyn says she is angry with herself.

FYI: Crossroads Counseling Center was one of the first private counseling centers to be licensed in the state of Wisconsin.

"I am so angry at my husband but I'm really angry at myself. I jumped from the frying pan into the blast furnace. I thought if I gave my husband enough love, he'd be OK. He was abused as a child and I thought all he needed was love. He said he'd change. He said he'd go to counseling. I don't know if I believe him. I feel paralyzed. I can't fix things anymore."

Marilyn's self-esteem is linked to her role as caretaker, a role that was placed on her shoulders at age nine. She was forced to prove her worth by taking care of other people. When she married a drunk with his own problems from childhood, she was traveling in a circle and unable to shed the mother's helper role she learned in childhood. As long as she was taking care of other people, there was

Tip: Many people find it is difficult to understand the differences in mental health counselors. I will explain the differences in mental health professionals in the State of Wisconsin. These definitions vary from state-to-state (See related tips on pages 55, 57, 58, 59 60 and 61).

Psychiatrists are MDs who have done postgraduate work in psychiatry. They do medical evaluations and supervision, and prescribe drugs. Typically, they do not do talk therapy. Clients who need prescription drugs see a psychiatrist every three months for a medical evaluation.

a structure to her life. Now, many years later, Marilyn is confronting her issues in the context of a marriage that isn't working. What saved her ass as a child is hanging her ass as an adult. Her pain is so great that she's ready to break through her issues by facing what happened in her youth.

> "I love my mother but she taught me by her example that I was not important. It was my father and my brothers who were important and I was their caretaker."

In therapy, I will continue to help Marilyn look at the role she's been playing and the other roles that she might choose. If Marilyn changes her role, she'll upset the equilibrium in her household. It takes two for the hero-rebel dynamic to work. Her husband will either have to change or leave.

Marilyn worked very hard on creating a new life. Al-Anon's[1] 12-step program helped Marilyn learn to set healthy boundaries. Ironically, her alcoholic husband developed so much stress from the changes that Marilyn introduced into their relationship that he entered a primary alcoholic treatment program. This came as a total surprise to Marilyn. She never thought he would seek help for his drinking problem. At the time of this writing, Marilyn and her husband are still attending Al-Anon and Alcoholics Anonymous (AA) and they're still together.

---

1 Al-Anon is a 12-step program for people with loved ones who are struggling with an addiction.

Breaking the Cycle of Dysfunction

Note:
People who walk through my door for therapy carry their family systems with them.

Therapists deal with family members even if they're not physically present. Identifying the connection between addictive or compulsive adult behavior and the events that took place in your childhood are two important steps for most people who seek counseling. Because the patterns of behavior in a family system are always carried into the future, healing, or breaking the cycle of dysfunction has the potential to alleviate your future struggles as a spouse or as a parent. On the road to healing, there are several important steps:

Step #1: Self-Examination

This step involves exploring the relationships in your childhood. Important questions to ask include:

- Did my family have secrets?
- Were the adults in my home abusive, neglectful or pervasively negative?

Adults who are stuck will need to do detective work to understand their family system (See: *Detective Work* in this chapter).

Step #2: Shed Your Dysfunctional Role

Leaving the family behind is a complex issue for a person who grows up in a dysfunctional family. It means shedding emotional baggage and moving ahead with your life as an independent human being. Important questions to ask include:

- Am I still overly bound to my family emotionally?
- Am I weighed down by guilt or shame from the events of my childhood?

Tip: Psychologists have a PhD or EdD (educational doctor). They do some talk therapy but a majority of their work is testing and supervision.

Shedding your role(s) from childhood is the key to getting unstuck. Although everyone's situation is unique, there are some general techniques that anyone can use (See: *Blending Your Roles* in this chapter).

Step #3: Grieving Your Loss

The grief process involves several stages. People who grew up in dysfunctional families need to grieve the loss of what they did not have. In her book *On Death and Dying*, Elisabeth Kubler-Ross identifies five patterns of emotional experience in the grieving process:

- Denial (this is not happening)
- Anger (why is this happening?)
- Bargaining (I promise I will be better if...)
- Depression (I don't care)
- Acceptance (I'm ready for whatever happens)

It is not unusual for my patients to get stuck in any one of the first four stages of grieving. They often don't know they're stuck but they realize what has happened when they begin therapy (See: *Gaining a Perspective on Loss and Change* in this chapter).

Step #4: Creating a New Life

This stage is one of the most important. It involves re-shaping your relationships or leaving toxic relationships behind (See: *Creating a New Life* later in this chapter).

Detective Work

Note:

People usually do not know they're stuck in a role from their childhood. An adult who is stuck is usually in pain because the role no longer works in their adult life. It takes detective work or self-examination to uncover the dynamics of your family system.

One of my goals in a counseling session is to help a client analyze their situation and reach conclusions on their own. Rather than tell Marilyn she's codependent, we worked on an exercise that's designed to help Marilyn determine:

- The role she may have played in her family

- If the role that saved her as a child is hanging her up as an adult

This exercise would require that Marilyn use her imagination and travel back to her early life in her family's household. All families develop rituals and patterns in their daily life and for Marilyn to study her family members, she would sit in a chair with her eyes closed and imagine a

Tip: A majority of the mental health counselors who do talk therapy hold a Masters degree. A smaller number are licensed but do not hold an advanced degree.

Masters degrees in counseling include:

- Masters in Counseling Psychology
- Masters in Guidance and Counseling

In the State of Wisconsin, a licensed professional counselor (LPC) is required to complete 3,000 hours of supervised work in a mental health facility after completing a Masters degree and passing the LPC exam.

scene from her childhood as though it was part of a movie. When Marilyn was in my office, I guided her through the creation of her scene with the following guided imagery (that readers may also use):

Visualize a Location

Imagine that your family members are together in some room of the house where you lived as a child. Your family members may be seated around a table, gathered together to watch television or at some family gathering. Note: Use a separate piece of paper to create a worksheet and make notes about the location of your movie.

Hear What They're Saying

As you create your family movie in your mind, imagine that you're recording something that each member has to say in keeping with his/her personality. Note: Record these statements on your worksheet.

Watch His/Her Physical Gestures

As you're filming the close-ups for your film, take note of each person's physical gestures. Are they:

- Happy or sad?
- Angry or fearful?
- Judgmental or critical?
- Quiet or talkative?

Note: Record these gestures on your worksheet.

Tip: Clinical Social Workers have a Masters degree in social work. In the State of Wisconsin, a licensed clinical social worker (LCSW) is required to complete 3,000 supervised hours of work in a mental health facility after completing their Masters degree and passing the LSCW exam.

Dysfunctional Family Deck

Use the following images to help determine if the characters in your family movie fit the classic roles that exist in a dysfunctional family system.

It's no accident that the cards in the family deck resemble images from the 600-year-old Tarot deck—cards that represent the quest for self-knowledge. We've made some changes in the Rider Waite drawings that are now in the public domain, but some of the original symbolism provides a pictorial language that is useful for this exercise.

These images may be photocopied and placed in front of you as you meditate and finish creating your movie:

THE ADDICT

THE ENABLER

THE HERO

THE REBEL

THE CLOWN

LOST CHILD

Tip: A licensed marriage and family therapist (LMFT) can have a graduate degree in:

- Counseling
- Psychology
- Social Work
- Counseling and Guidance

A license requires 3,000 hours of supervised work in a mental health facility and a passing grade on the LMFT exam.

The Principal Dysfunctional Member

The Principal Dysfunctional Member happens to be a male but the principal dysfunctional member could also be female. This person has an addiction to a drug, alcohol or compulsive behavior. He/she survived his/her own family trauma.

Symbolism:

Readers who are familiar with the Tarot deck will recognize the Devil—an addict who is represented by the goat-headed Pan, the Roman god of excess. Through lies and manipulation, this person holds chains that bind all the other members of the family.

Tip: Alcohol and drug counselors are required to be certified by the State of Wisconsin. This group includes:

- Registered Alcohol and Drug Counselor (RADC)
- Certified Alcohol and Drug Counselor (CADC, CADC II and CADC III)

This group is not required to have a bachelors although many have a bachelors, masters and sometimes a PhD. Candidates for an RADC certification must pass a test and file a plan of education with the state certification board (SCB). A CADC II and III must have this education completed as well as pass a written and oral test.

The Enabler

Enablers can be either male or female. They're usually a spouse who exhibits passive aggressive behavior. In other words, on the surface, it appears that the enabler is the one who is being controlled but in truth, they control passively.

Symbolism:

In the Enabler card we see a woman who is subduing a lion with her bare hands. Like the Strength card in the Tarot, she's involved in a difficult struggle. He or she is trying to tame or fix someone whose behavior is overwhelming. Later in the book, we'll learn that this person is a codependent personality who has low self-esteem.

Tip: Psychiatric Nurse
Therapists are required to have
a registered nurse's license
(R.N.), a Masters degree and
3,000 hours of supervised work
in a mental health facility.
Nurses can take advanced tests
to obtain an Advanced Practice
Psychiatric Nurse's License with
script rights. This group can
write prescriptions.

The Hero

The Hero always tries to make the family look good.
He gets straight As in school, he excels at sports and he
behaves like a parent to the other children.

THE HERO

Symbolism:

Like the Tarot's chariot driver, our hero is someone who
achieves mastery over everything that he/she attempts.
Although the hero appears to have successfully dealt with
his/her dysfunctional family, they are their own worst task
masters because they feel that they cannot fail.

FYI: I am licensed as a:

- Professional Counselor
- Social Worker
- Family Therapist

and I'm also certified as an Alcohol and Drug Counselor.

The Rebel

The rebel is usually blamed for the family pain. He's always in trouble, which creates stress in the family system. Family members blame the rebel. Blame is a form of denial and it's a sign that the family members do not want to see themselves. He does not consciously realize it, but his behavior is an attempt to get his parents to take action.

Symbolism:

With his (or her) feet half on land and half touching the water, the rebel tests or challenges everything that the world has to offer. The rebel has wings that appear on the angel figure in the Tarot deck's Temperance card. The wings and the dirt path in the background represents the fact that he/she often does not stick around for very long.

FYI: Although it is helpful to investigate your counselor's educational degree, your relationship with your counselor is more important. My advice is "trust your gut."

The Clown

The clown uses humor to relieve tension when the family pain becomes intense. Clowns usually have magnetic personalities and quick minds, reflecting a creativity that can light up a room.

THE CLOWN

Symbolism:

In the Tarot, there's an interesting connection between the clown/lunatic and the fool/joker. Throughout history, when freedom of speech was not permitted, lunatics were entitled to express themselves freely, to say things that others could not. In a dysfunctional family system that similarly forbids freedom of expression, the clown has the potential for speaking the most truth.

Quote: "We may have all come on different ships, but we're in the same boat now."

- Martin Luther King, Jr.

The Lost Child
The lost child likes to disappear into remote locations. It's his/her way of coping and escaping the pain of a dysfunctional family.

Symbolism:
Like the Hermit card in the Tarot deck, the lost child is isolated, preferring a private existence almost completely withdrawn from the world. The Tarot warns us that if we stay withdrawn for too long, growth stops. Like the Hermit, the Lost Child needs to rejoin the world.

Insights About Your Family

Sometimes, the first time you close your eyes to create your movie, insights about your family members will immediately seem apparent. Some of the roles may be easier to see than others and these are the "quick insights." Other roles may take more time to consider. If your family members don't seem to fit the classic roles found in dysfunctional family systems:

- Re-create your movie

- Review the directions for guided imagery presented in the beginning of this section as you do your visualization

- Think about the characters presented in this chapter and look for similarities

Sometimes roles may blend. For example, it is common for a hero child to also be a rebel. Sometimes clowns are also rebels.

Worksheet

Record your notes about your movie and characters on your worksheet.

Movie Location

Describe your movie's location:

Q & A: Have you ever wondered if you have a problem with alcohol? Look over the criteria presented below and on page 70 and consider if they apply to you:

1. Do you ever have blackouts and...

   - can't remember large portions of what happened when you were out drinking?

   - call your friends the next day to ask what happened?

   - wonder why your wife is mad the next day?

2. Is there alcoholism in your family? Are your mother, father, grandparents, siblings, aunts or uncles referred to as "heavy drinkers?"

Movie Characters—
What They're Saying and Their Gestures

Make a list of the characters (family members) in your movie and write down what they're saying as well as their physical gestures.

Blending Your Roles

Note:
Throughout life, the positive aspects of a role can be tapped and used in beneficial ways.

To help understand how roles hang people up, let's look at the extremes. The people who are profiled as positive have developed other skills and they have learned how to blend roles when necessary:

Rebel	Profile
Negative	Ends up in prison
Balanced	Often in detention but still gets good grades
Positive	Fights for social justice (e.g. Gandhi)

Hero	Profile
Negative	Surrounded by codependent relationships that he/she tries to fix.
Balanced	Takes care of family but has boundaries; navigates well at work
Positive	Successful leader (e.g. Jimmy Carter)

FYI: I am also nationally certified as a mental health counselor. I helped found the American Mental Health Counselors Association that does national certification. They are based in Washington, D.C.

Clown	Profile
Negative	Never serious, difficulties in school, too superficial
Balanced	Does really well at work; wife and family would like more substance
Positive	Jokester who helps society (e.g. Bill Cosby)

Lost Child	Profile
Negative	Totally isolated, never connects with anyone, no social skills, may drink alone or do drugs
Balanced	Has a job but is a loner (e.g. forest ranger, programmer)
Positive	Feels comfortable alone, has an ability to connect, has intimate connections with his/her family

Experimenting with Life's Opposite Roles

Getting unstuck involves balancing your roles or experimenting with life's opposite roles until you experience positive changes. As you try new roles, you'll develop new skills. Here are some classic examples:

Hero

Heroes are often enablers who take care of other people but have trouble asserting themselves. A hero who is willing to try out an opposite role might experiment by:

• sending unsatisfactory food back at a restaurant

• speaking up at work

• taking the night off from housework and cooking

• choosing a television program you want to watch

Rebel

Rebels are rule breakers who do not have a problem asserting themselves. A rebel who is willing to try out an opposite role might experiment by:

• taking up a social cause

• helping a neighbor

• volunteering for overtime

• listening and empathizing with someone in the family

Q & A: Have you ever wondered if you have a problem with alcohol? (continued from page 66):

3. Can you control your drinking? Do you go out for one or two drinks and end up closing the bar?

4. Do you have a personality change when you drink? Do people say, "she's a really nice person until she gets a few drinks in her and then she's 'hell on wheels.'" Or, "he's a crab unless he's drinking, then he is a teddy bear." Or, "Normally he's a shy guy, but he can get loud and obnoxious when he drinks."

If you answered "yes " to three or more of these questions, you may need alcohol and drug counseling.

Clown

Clowns have trouble behaving seriously whenever there is tension. A clown who is willing to try out an opposite role might experiment by:

• becoming a helper to a friend without cracking jokes

• volunteering at a senior citizen center

• starting a union in a non-union shop

Lost Child

Lost children have trouble joining in or participating. A lost child who is willing to try out an opposite might experiment by:

• starring in a play

• joining the board of directors of a nonprofit organization

• going to a dance and dancing

Gaining a Perspective on Loss and Change

Note:
Much of psychotherapy is about grieving because we work on change. It is natural for human beings to grieve what they have lost.

When you discover what happened to you in your family system, it's highly likely that you will experience grief. Typically, you will feel shock and disbelief. This is the first of several emotional stages described by Elisabeth Kubler-Ross in her grief model:

• Denial

• Anger

• Bargaining

• Depression

• Acceptance

Of all the research work done on grief, I'm particularly fond of Ken Moses' grief model. He explains that "grieving is an unlearned, spontaneous and self-sufficient process." The states in the Moses model are similar to Elisabeth Kubler-Ross' model:

• Denial

• Anxiety

• Fear

• Guilt

• Depression

Moses says that grieving occurs in "states" rather than stages, explaining that it is not a step-by-step process. For some, a state may be a short "blip" or some states may not occur at all. What's helpful about Ken Moses' model is his theory about the benefits that we gain in each of the states:

Tip: My first partner had his Ph.D. in counseling education and did his thesis on a counselor's ability to provide counseling. He learned that some of those who pursued advanced degrees beyond a Masters were less intuitive and not as good at therapy.

State	Benefit Described by Moses
Denial	"Buys the time needed to blunt the initial impact of the shattered dream and to discover the inner strength needed to confront what really happened."
Anxiety	"Mobilizes the energy needed to make changes."
Fear	"A warning that alerts a person to the seriousness of internal changes that are needed."
Guilt	"Guilt helps us redefine the issue of cause and responsibility in the light of loss. A guilt-ridden person accepts responsibility for everything. It feels better to do that than to believe that they have no influence on anything."

When we're faced with the need to change, we need mobilizing emotions. Anger is in the Kubler-Ross model and I would consider it to be another mobilizing force along with anxiety. It can be a mobilizing emotion if we use the energy of anger to take action.

Surviving grief can be a difficult experience. Here are some inspirational stories of people who used their mobilizing emotions to take positive action:

Quote: "Grief is essential for the adult child who is codependent, who needs powerfully and emotionally to grieve for all the things brought to awareness…"

- Dr. Robert Hemfelt et al.
Love is a Choice

Person Mobilized by His/Her Anger	Action
Cindy Sheehan California mother whose son died in Iraq.	Camped outside George Bush's Texas ranch demanding a face-to-face meeting so that she can ask about "the noble cause her son died for." Cindy's tenacity inspired antiwar demonstrators around the country to stage candlelight vigils.
Maureen Kanka New Jersey mother of nine year-old Megan Kanka, who was murdered by a sex offender.	Demanded a new law that would make sure police, neighbors, schools and municipal officials would be alerted when sex offenders are released from prison and when they move into residential neighborhoods. State Senator Peter Inverso, a Republican who lives in Hamilton Township where Megan was killed, took the lead in the legislature on the package of bills known collectively as Megan's Law that were signed into law in New Jersey by Governor Christie Whitman on Oct. 31, 1994 and later by then-President Bill Clinton requiring every state to adopt its own Megan's Law.

Quote: "We must learn to live together as brothers or perish together as fools."

- Martin Luther King, Jr.

Person Mobilized by His/Her Anger	Action
John and Revé Walsh Parents of six-year-Adam Walsh, who was kidnapped at a Sears store in Hollywood, Florida, and later murdered.	Led the fight for passage of the federal Missing Children's Act of 1982 and the federal Missing Children's Assistance Act of 1984. The latter legislation created the National Center for Missing and Exploited Children, which maintains a toll-free hotline number (800-THE-LOST) to report a missing child or the sighting of one. John Walsh later became the host of *America's Most Wanted*, a television show that aired for 12 years and helped apprehend more than 600 fugitives.

Creating a New Life

Note:
The process of creating a new life is a journey. Learn to be patient with yourself and understand that learning new skills takes time.

This is one of the most important stages of healing. For some, it may feel like waking up from a long sleep. Read on to learn some strategies for reshaping a dysfunctional life:

Work on Detaching Your Emotions

This step is about as hard as having your leg amputated without anesthesia, but unhooking your emotions is necessary for healing. Here are some points to consider:

Create a Survival Strategy for Your Relationship
It's critical that you don't fall into the fantasy that you have a normal family. This requires that you constantly remind yourself that they're dysfunctional. It may also require that you:

• limit the amount of time you spend with them

• avoid topics that trigger you

• bring a supportive friend or partner with you when you visit

Appreciate That You're Awake
You woke up and it's time to cut your losses. Your opportunity to reshape your life is a gift. Realize that many people will never wake up.

Intellectual Understanding Helps Provide Closure
Your awareness of what took place in your childhood is a turning point. Realize that the rest of your life is precious and that letting go of the past is critical if you want to successfully start over. Don't get stuck in the grieving process because it will weigh you down as you create your new beginning.

Quote: "Parents need help. We don't have all the answers and engage in power trips."

- John Bradshaw
Creating Love

Stop Blaming Your Family

Resist the urge to blame your family and see them as members of their own dysfunctional families who never had a chance to heal. Here are some points to consider:

Your Abusers are Children with Unmet Needs
If your family members never healed, it means that they stopped growing emotionally. The damage may be severe and they may have the emotional development of a very young child.

Try Not to Slip into Denial
When you forget about your family's dysfunction, you slip into denial. Resist believing in the fantasy that they're normal. Be proud that you're different and that you've made the decision to heal.

Experience an Emotional Catharsis and Move On
Talking about what happened helps us mourn, and it's considered an emotional catharsis or release. Realize that your experiences will probably always hurt, but if you want to create a new life you will need to think about the future and not the past.

Set New Boundaries

A person's ability to create or respect boundaries is something that is learned in childhood. In dysfunctional families, there may be no boundaries or formidable boundaries that are total barriers. At times, conditions fluctuate with extremes existing in the same families. Distorted ideas about boundary issues such as privacy, personal respect, and rights arise because boundaries are interpreted as a rejection. And in dysfunctional families, there is a

Quote: "In order to succeed, your desire for success should be greater than your fear of failure."

- Bill Cosby
Comedian

tremendous fear of rejection. Here are some points to consider:

Self-assertion is the Key to Setting Boundaries
To be self-assertive, you will need to overcome your fear of rejection and not being liked or wanted. In a dysfunctional family, children frequently ARE rejected and they never learn about healthy boundaries. It's important to learn that a physical, psychological or emotional boundary has nothing to do with rejection and that they are a healthy and necessary part of life.

Dysfunctional Families Will Not Want You to Heal
Rigid family systems do not adapt to change. If your family reacts negatively when you start to heal— that's a good thing. I frequently tell patients to be prepared for outbursts and negative reactions from family members while they're seeing a psychotherapist.

Meet Eddie

Note:
Eddie is an example of someone who is able to 'shape-shift' in the outside world. Every healthy adult should have several roles to choose from—and not just one or two.

Roles exist because there is trauma. In households where there are a lot of painful experiences, the roles that exist are very rigid. In healthy households, roles are temporary and "choiceful." The emotional environment is flexible and always yielding to change. Unfortunately, most people come from dysfunctional families. It is estimated that eighty-to-ninety percent of households have problems that may be called dysfunctional.

Although it would be nice to be able to turn back the clock and undo the events of our childhood, that's not possible. Ideally, as adults, those who survive their childhood by depending on one or more life-saving roles learn to safely put away their roles. Putting away the roles that saved your ass in childhood doesn't mean you'll never use them again. There may be a circumstance that will require you to shape-shift and draw on what you learned in your childhood role.

A friend of mine who is an actor was a rebel child in his youth. Eddie grew up on the South Side of Chicago and at 18, he managed to meet friends who helped transform him into a supermodel.

When I met Eddie, he was twenty and he had lost all the rough edges that helped him survive Chicago's worst neighborhoods. His clothes, his speech and his mannerisms gave the impression that he came from a privileged family. He had successfully shape-shifted and had erased all traces of the street. His real goal was to become an actor and as far as I was concerned, he was already exhibiting his skill. When I visited him, he had joined the cast of a small theater group in Chicago.

Quote: "Soulfulness is characterized by freedom. When we live soulfully, we choose our own life projects."

- John Bradshaw
Creating Love

When Eddie's show opened, I went to see his play and we took the train back to his apartment late that night. On the train platform, Eddie had an opportunity to pull out the "rebel." We each had dates that night and while we all waited for the train, two rough-looking men approached our dates who were standing and talking several feet away from us on the platform. Eddie reacted, and his rebel child was so fierce that the two men stepped up their pace and kept walking. I had never seen Eddie's rebel and I never forgot what happened that night. Putting away your life-saving roles for safekeeping is exactly what's needed as an adult. All of what Eddie learned to survive his youth is helpful—but only in appropriate circumstances. To succeed professionally, Eddie needed to bury the rebel and adopt new and appropriate roles in his day-to-day life.

Meet Alice

Note:

My patients give me a lot of hope concerning how strong we are as human beings. I'm always amazed at children who survive negative situations and turn out to be caring human beings who want to make the world a better place.

Sometimes patients find it easier to write out their thoughts. These can then be used as a springboard for our face-to-face sessions. As you can see in Alice's journal, she proved to be quite a poignant author.

One of the saddest aspects of alcohol and drug abuse is the physical and emotional pattern of neglect that occurs when an addict has children. The children who live with an addict often raise themselves and survive by adopting the roles that I described in the first chapter. Alice, age 45, is an example. She first came to see me at age 34. Every one of the adults in her family was an alcoholic and she faced the reality of her difficult youth as a hero child. When I first met Alice eleven years ago, I encouraged her to write a journal reflecting her childhood memories at different ages, and here are four of the entries.

Little Girl Without a Bed (an Infant)

Alice's alcoholic parents constantly left her alone with other adults who were not responsible:

Beach Cot Alice

Alice is a baby
somewhere she has a crib
but she isn't somewhere
she is nowhere

nowhere, limbo
not here
not there
nowhere

not with Mommy
not with Daddy
not asleep in a crib

put to sleep in a buggy
harnessed "for safety's sake"

Quote: "All our dreams can come true, if we have the courage to pursue them."

- Walt Disney

What are they thinking of
putting Alice to sleep in a harness?

Are the dreams of a harnessed baby
the same as the dreams of a baby tucked into her crib?
Alice doesn't think so.

one night Alice awakes harnessed in her buggy
a beautiful baby
a precious gift from God
She can't dream the dreams of a harnessed baby any longer.

she deserves her Mommy
she deserves her Daddy
she deserves to be tucked into her crib

someone
not her Mommy
not her Daddy
wakes and finds Alice dangling from the side of her buggy

harnessed "for safety's sake"
turning blue
gasping for air
twisted and tangled in the safety harness

Alice survives and grows into a beautiful little girl
a precious gift from God

somewere she has a bed
but she isn't somewhere
she is nowhere

nowhere, limbo
not here
not there
nowhere

Quote: "Only as high as I reach can I grow, Only as far as I seek can I go, Only as deep as I look can I see, Only as much as I dream can I be."

Karen Ravn
Author
Our Inward Journey

Alice Meets The Three-Legged Uncle (Age 6)

Alice experienced nonstop trauma through her childhood, as we see in her journal entry about an experience at age six:

Alice was moving. She wasn't sure what to think of that. It didn't matter what she thought of it anyway. She was moving. Everyone else seemed to be acting like it was a good thing so Alice decided to think of it as a good thing. Besides, they kept talking about the new place being bigger. The place where Alice slept was three rooms with five people. There was a living room, kitchen and one bedroom. The place where Mary Ann slept had four rooms with five people. A living room, kitchen and two bedrooms which meant Mary Ann had her own room. It was very little, just big enough for a single bed. When Alice slept over she and Mary Ann slept together in the single bed and Alice liked sleeping in a real bed with another person. Then in the morning Mary Ann's brothers and Mary Ann would play "Doctors" and operate on Alice. All Alice remembers about that game is all the doctors start to touch her and that then she floated away to "La-La Land." When Alice returned from her private world, La-La Land, the others would be in the kitchen eating Cheerios.

Alice kept hearing the adults say, "five rooms." She did the math and concluded she was getting a room just like Mary Ann. She also concluded that in her room she wouldn't allow any game of "Doctors." Moving day came. Finally she would see the place. She just couldn't understand it. Why would anyplace need two living rooms? What were poor people going to do with a parlor? Alice was disappointed to learn that a parlor was a room full of furniture that she wasn't allowed to touch.

Quote: "What's the sense of having a spine if you're not going to use it?"
- Tour Guide
Red Rock Tours
Sedona, Arizona

Eventually it was bedtime and Alice was excited to learn she was going to be sleeping in a bed with her Great Aunt and Great Uncle. There wasn't much room squished between two large adults in a full-size bed, but Alice was in a bed in a bedroom and she liked it. Then her uncle started to test her knowledge. Alice was smart so she didn't mind his questions—until he insisted she was wrong when she answered, "two" when asked how many legs her uncle had. To prove his point the uncle took Alice's hand and had her count the legs under the sheet, "One, two, three." When Alice counted leg number two her stomach flipped like when the stitches dissolved after her tonsilectomy. Boy, that was a mess.

The room went totally silent. The kind of silence that hurts your ears. Alice realized that mattress had turned to a solid block of ice. She was cold beyond shivers. Alice decided it was time to float away to La-La Land, but the air in the room was so heavy it was like a hand that kept her in place. Her aunt was asking the uncle what he had done and he was proudly declaring his answer.

The next night Alice got a sheet and was told to go to sleep on the armless couch in the living room. Alice did what she was told.

The Miracle of Birth (Age 12)

Alice's journal entry about her life at age 12 reveals her hero child behavior.

The miracle of birth...
She was beautiful.
I gazed lovingly into her clear blue eyes
And she looked into mine.
I could never have imagined such a moment.

Then years passed
And through no fault of my own, we were apart too often.

I worried.
I worried when we were apart
And I worried when we were together, too.

Almost 12 years after that miraculous day
Find me pacing.
As I move across the room
I wring my hands
And pray she is alright.

Why doesn't she call?
How can she stay out all night?
How can I take care of her when she isn't even home?

I continue to pace.
I continue to pray.

I pray for her.
I pray for the one I call "Mother."

Quote: "One of the things I learned the hard way was that it doesn't pay to get discouraged. Keeping busy and making optimism a way of life can restore your faith in yourself."

- Lucille Ball

Alice's Rebel

Alice's predominant childhood role was that of a hero child. However, there were times when she drew on her rebel role, as illustrated in this journal entry:

"My brother and I got kicked out of our private schools. There was an issue of tuition nonpayment. We never knew for sure who our benefactor was who paid for over four years of boarding school, but he wasn't paying anymore.

My brother went to live with our Great Aunt and Great Uncle. I was supposed to go there, too, but I insisted on going to live with my mother. I knew she needed someone to take care of her and I knew that job was mine.

What I didn't know was, during my years away my mother got used to not being expected to act like a mother. So, I spent day after day and night after night alone in a one-room apartment in a transient building in one of Chicago's "changing neighborhoods." I was twelve years old.

Then one night I heard the three quick rings of the doorbell. That meant there was a phone call in the lobby. I was up on the third floor. I knew it wasn't safe for me to go out of the locked apartment, but I feared my mother might be the one calling me—she might be in trouble, she might need me. So, I buzzed back to let the manager know I was coming to take the call.

I was surprised by the voice on the phone. It wasn't the police or an ambulance driver calling about my mother. It was a nun. She explained she was the principal at the

Quote: "Human beings can alter their lives by altering their attitudes of mind."

- William James
  American Philosopher

Catholic school and that my mother had called to enroll me. (I wondered what had happened that got my mother to finally make that call. She never seemed to notice that I was even in that room.)

Sister asked why my mother wasn't the one who came to take the call. I thought about the answer the good daughter was expected to give. Then I thought about the last weeks of sitting alone waiting to take care of my absent mother. Without any emotion I simply uttered, "My mother goes out. I'm all alone." Sister simply replied, "Oh." Then she told me to be at school the next morning.

I literally marched back to my room, set my hair on my pink rollers, laid out my clothes as instructed by the nuns at boarding school, wound the clock, and set the alarm. When the alarm sounded, I started getting ready and while I was ironing my white, Catholic-schoolgirl blouse, my mother tried sneaking in. She was expecting me to be asleep so she could pretend she had been there all night. This morning I wasn't pretending to be asleep so that her charade could continue. With her plan foiled she became angry and snapped, "What are you doing?"

It was the first time I remember standing so straight and the first time I was aware that I wasn't speaking to this woman, who was three times my age, as my mother but as my rebellious teenage daughter. I looked her in the eye and I told her with attitude I never knew I had, "Sister called. I told her you went out. I told her you left me all alone. Now, I am getting ready to go to my new school." I spoke these words as the twelve year old

mother of a thirty-six year old teenager. The thirty-six year old teenager simply replied, "Oh."

Hero Children Often Struggle With Hypervigilance

She also grew up with a pervasive feeling of fear because of the repetitive traumas that she experienced. She played the role of "Mom" at age twelve and never had a childhood. As adults, hero children feel as though there's a need to work at being perfect. They're so used to the hard work that's required to keep up their dysfunctional family's false front that they never really relax. In her case, Alice grew up feeling as though she was keeping the family together.

Trauma of a Lost Childhood

Hypervigilance among hero children is very common and not all that dissimilar to the Post Traumatic Stress Disorder (PTSD) experienced by survivors who have witnessed death due to a sudden or traumatic accident or disaster. The American Psychiatric Association's Diagnostic and *Statistical Manual of Mental Disorders*, Fourth Edition (DSM-IV) describes the following characteristics:

1. The person experienced, witnessed or was confronted with an event or events that involved actual or threatened death or serious injury, or a threat to the physical integrity of self or others.

2. The person's response involved intense fear, helplessness or horror.

Traumatic Grief

In the past several years, mental health professionals have started to see a relationship between grief and the stress response associated with trauma. The similarities have caused therapists to invent the term *traumatic grief* to describe behavior that lingers much longer than the grief associated with the loss of a significant other but not as long as the behavior associated with PTSD. The National Institute for Trauma and Loss in Children has constructed a chart to describe traumatic grief. I have listed that part of the chart that describes behavior following a loss that is not necessarily a death:

Grief/Bereavement	Traumatic Grief	PTSD
Single Incident	Multiple incidents	Multiple incidents
Pangs of grief	Hypervigilance	Preoccupation with terror/ horror inducing elements of the incident
Intense yearning	Feeling of futility about the future	Avoidance prominent
Seeks out familiar places/ persons	Shattered worldview	Feelings of futility about the future
Able to maintain interests, experience pleasure	Excessive irritability, bitterness or anger	Focuses on elements of horror and terror

Grief/Bereavement	Traumatic Grief	PTSD
Accepts death and moves forward	Prolonged impaired social/ occupational functioning	Shattered worldview
		Excessive irritability, bitterness, anger related to overwhelming sense of powerlessness and/or absence of a sense of safety
		Cognitive dysfunction—difficulty attending, focusing, retaining, recalling and processing verbal information
		Prolonged impaired social/ occupational functioning

Taking the Temperature of a Room

In some ways, Alice still shows signs of her traumatic grief over the loss of her childhood. She's extremely hypervigilant and has an extreme need to feel safe. In her day-to-day experiences, she has a need to know exactly who and what she will be dealing with. She calls it, "taking the temperature of a room."

Quote: "Mistakes are a part of being human. Appreciate your mistakes for what they are: precious life lessons that can only be learned the hard way. Unless it's a fatal mistake, which, at least, others can learn from."

- Al Franken

Ken Moses' Grief Model

As people become aware of what happened to them in their youth, they will need to deal with their emotions over the loss of their childhood and they will need to grieve. In Chapter 1, we covered the Ken Moses grief model that is very similar to Elisabeth Kubler-Ross' well-known model. I mentioned that I like Moses' theory about the states that may not occur in any particular order as well as the benefits that we gain in each of the states (See: "Gaining a Perspective on Loss and Change").

Chapter 2

RULE #2

The Things People Say to Themselves I Would Not Say to My Worst Enemy

Each person's reality is based on his/her belief system.
Love and respect (for ourselves) can promote healing, but necessary ingredients include:

• an understanding concerning the events that took place in our childhood
• diligent re-programming

"In this chapter, we'll discuss one of the most important concepts in mental health—that life is about choices and that our beliefs about ourselves create our reality.

Unfortunately, most of us spend a lifetime struggling with the programming we endured in our youth. Behavioral researchers tell us that most of what we think about ourselves is negative and that the scripts were mostly written when we were very young.

Although parents are responsible for nurturing and caring for their children, they are often incapable of creating the kind and loving scripts that are needed because they are products of their own early programming. To understand this, we'll explore what are generally accepted as basic human needs and use a scorecard to see if we can find a relationship between early caretaker behavior and what we believe about ourselves. The scorecard can be used to assess any authority that seeks to program our thinking (parents, teachers, friends, the church or even government)."

What Happened in Your Childhood?

Note:
We need to constantly remind ourselves that we are free to make choices and that the limits we experience in life are often self-imposed.

Hal Ashley's film Being There is a satire about a man who has lived all of his adult life inside a townhouse and walled garden. Because he is a WASP, middle-aged and well-groomed, he is automatically assumed to be a person of substance. The joke is that he is really someone who has been programmed to conduct well-bred conversations. The film's last line is very true— 'Life is a state of mind.' Often, there are many things in life that are not what they seem.

Every character in the films I will mention in this book has a detailed backstory that establishes how the character's world manifests. Screenwriters develop a detailed backstory for each of their characters even before they start writing their script (the more detailed the better). Our detective work concerning what happened in our childhoods can help us understand why we behave the way that we do.

Childhood Abuse Causes Distorted Views

This year's show called *Supernanny* was a hit in the UK before it migrated to ABC prime time in the United States. Jo Frost, who's a real nanny, helps troubled families with unruly children. The show's families are at the no-routine, no-boundaries and no-discipline end of the child-rearing spectrum that may be due to clueless parents—or, passive abuse.

At the other end of the child-rearing spectrum are the active abusers—the group that has been taught to tame children with severe and often brutal practices. Our society has been programmed to believe that human beings must be controlled, and the concept is reinforced over and over. Although this belief is slowly being replaced with the idea that an individual deserves respect from birth, abuse is still prevalent in many cultures, leading to misery, poverty, war and brutality.

Basic Human Needs

Respect for other human beings begins with ourselves and anything less is a betrayal of our humanity.

Let's explore the concept of respect a little further by examining basic human needs. The most famous theory of human needs belongs to psychologist Abraham Maslow.

His "Hierarchy of Human Needs" is often presented as a pyramid. Maslow theorized that human beings make progress as they move up the pyramid. Physiological needs, or those that are needed for survival, are presented at the base of the pyramid. Maslow felt that once the most basic needs are taken care of, a person is able to concentrate on each new level in the hierarchy—moving up and working on each subsequent level of needs as each previous level is fulfilled.

International researchers have recently modified Maslow's Hierarchy of Needs to include nine basic needs that each have positive and negative behavior outcomes when the needs are met or unmet. When people do not get their needs met, they are driven to negative behavior. Manfred Max-Neef, a Chilian economist who taught at the University of California at Berkeley, is responsible for developing the nine basic human needs that are part of his Human Scale Development model. The following chart presents the Manfred Max-Neef human needs as well as the resulting positive and negative behavior outcomes. I've added a few extra dimensions, including:

• Positive contributing adult behavior

• Negative contributing adult behavior

Manfred Max-Neef Nine Basic Human Needs	Positive Contributing Parent Behavior	Positive Behavior When Needs Are Met
Subsistence	Children are given proper nutrition and do not over or undereat. They have clothes that are appropriate to the environment and there is a predictable pattern to child-care. Parents who are not naturally organized may need help with scheduling.	Feels safe, connected and secure. Everything will be OK.
Protection	Parents rely on boundaries and ordered predictable patterns to communicate what's expected. They use discipline (mixed with praise when there are positives) instead of harsh punishment to maintain firm but fair control. The home is toddler-proofed as a child grows, and older children are taught proper (safe) limits.	Feels protected from all major threats to the body and spirit.
Affection	Parents realize that children need age-appropriate affection and healthy touches all their life. They never let a day go by without a hug and a kiss.	Feels a need for interpersonal relationships that include warmth and intimacy.

Negative Contributing Parent Behavior	Negative Behavior When Needs Are Not Met	Note
Parent(s) may have been an alcoholic incapable of providing the necessities of life. Physical abuse or abandonment.	Overly cautious, fearful. Damage to self-esteem causes a person to feel shame. Children of alcoholics often marry alcoholics.	Physical and emotional abuse is one of the most negative childhood experiences. Adults who were abused as children may use alcohol or drugs as an escape.
Parent may have left child alone or was sick or possibly died. Parent may have been unstable due to depression or alcohol. Parent may have also been overinvolved in child's life.	Does not trust and is hypervigilant. Never feels safe. Often repeats this pattern with self-destructive relationships as an adult (e.g. abused children marry abusive spouses). People who were over-protected may feel abandoned as adults. They may also choose partners who have problems with commitment.	Over-protective parents may have fears about health, safety or poverty that they inherited from their parents. Chronic anxiety due to a person's fear may manifest as health problems.
No physical affection or emotionally distant. Parents may have quarreled frequently, they may have been overly critical or controlled children by withdrawing affection.	Avoids intimacy because it feels unfamiliar and uncomfortable. Feels unworthy of love and is emotionally disconnected.	Human nature causes us to repeat negative patterns. People who were abused often blame themselves for the abuse. They may also have problems saying "no."

Needs (continued)	Positive Contributing Adult Behavior	Positive Behavior When Needs Are Met
Understanding	Positive parents understand that young children like routines and consistency. They focus on children's positive traits, they listen to them, give them consistent time and attention. These parents understand that you cannot buy love and that staying actively involved in their childrens' lives is important.	Feels a deep need for acceptance and interconnectedness that comes through shared life experiences.
Participation	*Secret Life of Supermom* author Kathy Buckworth advises that eating together counts. A lot of positive interaction can occur at meals.	Has a desire to be involved in life.
Idleness	Positive parents know that the quality of life is not linked to money or a perfectly clean house.	Takes time to relax, reflect, heal and recreate.

Negative Contributing Parent Behavior	Negative Behavior When Needs Are Not Met	Note
Parents may have treated child as an object. Parent(s) may have been: • controlling • absent or unable to connect Parents may have been liars or manipulators and failed to validate a child's feelings.	Envious, jealous, xenophobic (fear of different classes of people). Has trouble relating emotionally because there were no early emotional connections made. May have difficulty expressing needs. Emotionally deprived children may compensate by becoming demanding as adults.	Physical or emotional deprivation may be due to a parent's alcoholism or a drug addiction. It can also be due to a personality disorder that will be discussed later in the book (e.g., narcissist, borderline personality disorder or antisocial).
Parent(s) may have been: • disinterested in their children • emotionally out-of-sync	Confusion, loss, feels abandoned, betrayed. Avoids social get-togethers. Feels isolated.	People need frequent homework assignments to re-program their thinking.
Parents may have dominated every aspect of family life. Parents may have denied their own needs.	Cannot relax and enjoy life. May limit social interaction.	By now, you can see how negative patterns in a person's youth are related to early programming and a person's beliefs about themselves.

Needs (continued)	Positive Contributing Adult Behavior	Positive Behavior When Needs Are Met
Creation	Parents expose children to a variety of different experiences to search for their likes or dislikes. They are supportive if a child is drawn to interests different from their own.	Feels a need to innovate and explore one's potential.
Identity	Parents communicate a child's worth by providing attention and praise as well as realistic, age-appropriate feedback.	Has a need to belong to a family, peer group or community.
Freedom	Parents explain rules or routines to children. They're straightforward and detailed so that children understand what is expected. Freedom increases as a child's skills increase.	Has a requirement for action without stifling restrictions on one's space, time and consciousness.
Transcendence	Parents take responsibility for their actions and do not blame others. They are emotionally mature and practice patience, kindness and cooperation.	Has a need to find an ultimate reality that gives meaning to life.

Negative Contributing Parent Behavior	Negative Behavior When Needs Are Not Met	Note
Parents may have been critical or forced a child into activities because of their own interests. One or more parent may have felt threatened by or jealous of their child.	Not confident about talent or intelligence. Parents made their child feel inadequate and may have been negative in making comparisons to a brother or sister.	People who feel worthless may compensate with drugs, alcohol, food or work.
Parents may have humiliated a child or projected their own fear giving the child little or no responsibility.	Overly accommodating, feels weak and passive. Feels shame but goes to great lengths to hide these feelings. Feels unworthy of respect and hides aspects of himself or herself to fit in.	People who were abused as children may feel the need to defend their parents. In reality, they need to confront the feelings they experienced as children in order to heal.
Parent(s) make every decision and are never apart from their child. The child is never allowed an opinion. Alternatively, there are no limits and the child raises himself/herself.	Feels controlled or has no respect for authority. Life may revolve around work. May feel pressured to attain success. May feel angry and may disguise anger by being passive-aggressive.	Children who raise themselves and have no limits do not trust adults. They feel equal to adults at an early age and as a result, they have no respect for authority.
Finding the meaning of life is usually an adult pursuit that may be difficult if a person is still struggling with negative patterns.	Feels disillusioned later in life, unable to face pain, may develop an addiction.	Later, we'll cover techniques that you can use to reprogram negative early conditioning.

Parent (or Caregiver) Scorecard

Note:
One of the reasons people feel the need to defend their parents is because they may have been good parents in many ways. For example, it's possible they were good providers in a material sense but were very aloof and detached emotionally. The objective of this section is not to crucify your parents, but to understand the negative patterns (or beliefs) of your youth so you can reprogram your thinking.

We all learned our mental programming early and unless we break our negative patterns, we'll end up passing the same programming on to our children—or feeling disillusioned later in life.

Strangely, our negative self-defeating thoughts about ourselves often go unnoticed. They're often passed along from generation to generation. Examples include:

"Why can't you be like your brother?"

"You never listen."

"You talk too much."

"You're selfish."

These are just a few examples of verbal programming. There are many more examples of behavior programming that's subtle but just as damaging.

Steps for Grading Your Parent (or Some Other Adult)

This section includes a report card designed to help you understand the areas where your parents excelled and the areas where they had shortcomings. Give each parent an A, B, C, D or F in each category.

Material

Food
_____

Shelter
_____

Clothing
_____

Safety
_____

Emotional Connections

Ability to Express Love
_____

Ability to Show Respect
_____

Ability to Cope with Life Stress
_____

Emotional Maturity
_____

Stability
_____

Consistency
_____

Closeness
_____

Connectedness
_____

Trustworthiness
_____

Self-Esteem

Ability to Show Encouragement/Praise
_____

Ability to Guide
_____

Discipline/Responsibility

Overprotective
_____

Underprotective
_____

Practical Guidance
_____

What If One or Both Parents Has a D or an F?

My guess is that parents' scores will follow a bell curve just like grades in school. In most cases, parents will get average marks, with some As balancing out the Fs. When a parent with problems marries a more stable loving partner,

FYI: In his book *Creating Love*, author John Bradshaw recounts how he had a deep sense of depression and failure about his marriage and family at age 55 when he was single and all his children were grown and gone. He spent a lot of time thinking of how the dinner table was never a scene of deep attentive sharing as he had dreamed. When he shared this with a male support group, several others reported having the same disappointment. One guy asked, "Did any of you actually experience any of this in your families growing up?" Not one person could answer yes. John said he probed his memory and realized he had picked up that fantasy from watching shows like *Ozzie and Harriet* and *Leave It to Beaver*.

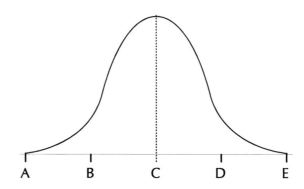

a child benefits from the love and support of one parent. The adults who have the most work to do are those with:

• one parent with several low scores

• both parents with several low scores

What Happens Next?

If you gave one or both parents several low scores, you have taken a significant step forward. It is often very hard for people who lived with abuse to face the truth. However, if you don't confront the past, it will be impossible to heal. Confronting the past is just the beginning. As we saw in the Manfred Max-Neef Human Development Model, people with unmet needs are driven to negative behavior that is often based on negative thought patterns. Abuse and neglect inflict similar wounds, and it might be said that a lack of self-love or self-esteem is at the base of all of the negative patterns.

The Devil You Know...

Before they heal, young men and women who experience abuse often attract abusive partners. For example, the

FYI: There's an ad in Oprah's magazine opposite Janine Latus' article. It contains a photo of Salma Hayek, who's a spokesperson for the Avon Foundation's Speak Out Against Domestic Violence campaign. Beneath her picture is this quote:

"We cannot tolerate a world in which one in three women is a victim of domestic violence. Please support my partnership with the Avon Foundation to end domestic violence. Speak Out So it Stops!"

> \- Salma Hayek
> Actress

October 2005 issue of Oprah Winfrey's *O* Magazine contains a chilling story titled "All the Wrong Men." Author Janine Latus describes how she and her sister spent years attaching themselves to controlling, verbally abusive men. Unfortunately, verbal abuse was familiar—their father was controlling and abusive. Throughout their life, Janine and her sister also ignored their instincts about the men in their lives—a topic we will discuss later in the book. Janine broke the pattern before the abuse became too dangerous; Amy didn't. Her husband went too far and her body was recovered three years later.

People who grow up with abuse are often in the dark about the characteristics of a normal relationship and may accept abuse from many people in their lives—partners, friends and possibly bosses.

In the next section, I've created a scorecard for friends and partners. It's similar to the parent scorecard and designed to help you identify unacceptable behavior in your adult relationships.

Partner, Friend or Boss Scorecard

Note:

No one is perfect but some people have more negative programming than others. If you have one or more negative people in your circle, it's important to know how much influence they have on your own mental programming.

The partner, friend or boss scorecard in this section may be more challenging than the parent scorecard because it's very common for abused people to cling to familiar patterns. They have no frame of reference for what's normal. If parents do not isolate their children, it's possible that they have gathered clues at their friends' homes or from television.

If you're one of the unfortunate people who were totally surrounded by dysfunctional people, it may take some time to learn what's normal. If you've attracted people into your life with similar patterns, you may need to make some changes in your personal relationships.

Steps for Grading the People in Your Life

Think of someone in your life who you would like to grade. Provide an A, B, C, D or F for each of the following categories:

Material

Although partners, friends and bosses do not provide the same type of critical life support as parents, life is a two-way street based on equal exchanges of energy. This category should not really be about money because people have unequal wealth. Instead of focusing on material possessions or money, try to think about whether the people in your life practice reciprocity. Use the following questions as a guide and write a grade in the space provided:

Quote: "When does a practicing alcoholic or drug addict lie?

Whenever he/she opens his/her mouth."

- Marv Wopat
Employee
Assistance
Program
General Motors

[Partner or Friend] Does he/she know your favorite food(s), music or TV shows?

[Partner, Friend or Boss] Is he/she familiar with your personal needs (e.g., alone time, health requirements or family responsibilities?)

[Partner or Boss] Does he/she protect you from nasty in-laws, office politics or unreasonable work assignments?

[Partner, Friend or Boss] Is he/she interested in your career advancement?

Emotional Connections

[Partner or Friend] Does he/she ever seem jealous?

[Partner, Friend or Boss] Does he/she include you in meetings or events with other colleagues or friends?

[Partner or Friend] Does he/she ever seem possessive?

[Partner, Friend or Boss] Does he/she ever seem critical or controlling?

[Partner, Friend or Boss] Is he/she trustworthy?

[Partner, Friend or Boss] Have you ever caught him/her in a lie?
[Partner, Friend or Boss] Can you count on him/her to do the right thing?
[Partner, Friend or Boss] Have you ever thought of his/her behavior as childish?
[Partner, Friend or Boss] Is he/she selfish?

Out With the Old, In With the New

Chances are, if you have negative people in your circle who were abused themselves, they're helping to reinforce your destructive thought patterns about yourself.

If anyone in your circle received several failing grades, you know what you need to do. When we take care of ourselves in appropriate ways, the universe has a funny way of filling in the gaps. It's a universal principle that's a lot like pruning a plant. When you remove leaves in strategic places, the plant experiences super growth. This won't occur until you take steps to prune. People who were abused early in their life will usually need to do a lot of pruning in their relationships.

In *Gardening for Dummies*, author Mike MacCashey calls pruning, "Cutting to redirect the plant's growth to where you want it." He says, "It may be a big job, like removing a heavy, damaged limb, or it may involve the simple removal of a spent flower. It's part maintenance, part preventative medicine and part landscaping." In his book, *Jerry Baker's Old-Time Gardening Wisdom*, Jerry describes "proper pruning":

> "From the second year on, we kept Grandma Putt's bushes well pruned."

If Jerry pruned his blackberry bushes every year to keep them healthy, you owe it to your self to "snip off" any "dead relationships" for good mental health.

Pruning Can Be Done With Detachment

Separating yourself from negative people can be done physically or mentally. If it's impossible to separate yourself physically from the negative people in your life, it helps to remind yourself:

• They are children with unmet needs

• Their negative behavior is due to immaturity

How We Feel About Ourselves

Our attitudes about life affect how we feel about ourselves. Here are some attitudes about life that will help form positive thoughts:

We Are Responsible for Our Thoughts, Our Actions and Our Happiness

You have the power to choose all thoughts, words and actions. No one else can upset you—you upset yourself. Your power lies within unless you give it away. Freedom comes with responsibility. We experience greater and greater freedom when we become more responsible.

Quote: "It's toughest to forgive ourselves. So it's probably best to start with other people. It's almost like peeling an onion. Layer by layer, forgiving others, you really do get to the point where you can forgive yourself."

- Patty Duke
  Actress

Redirection of Negative Self-Talk Takes Diligence

We are in charge of our own thoughts. We all have negative thought patterns running through our subconscious and as these thoughts rise to the surface, we can consciously redirect the thought energy in a positive direction.

We Need to Give Love Rather Than Get Love

Mature love is a shared positive energy. True love is a connection to the Divine that we carry and share with others.

There are No Excuses for Disrespect or Exploitation

There is a shared opinion among all religious, ethical groups and philosophies that we need to treat others in a decent manner. In Christianity, it's referred to as the *Golden Rule:* "Do unto others as you would have them do unto you." This is a very ancient principle that is related to the *Law of One,* meaning that what we do to others, we do to ourselves. Christ often expressed this as *one body:*

1 Corinthians 12:13 For by one Spirit we were all baptized into one body whether Jews or Greeks, whether slaves or free, and we were all made to drink of one Spirit.

No One Owes Us Anything

We are in charge of our own life. Feeling "owed" creates a lack of consciousness that is distracting and often causes us to look at life as though it were "half-empty." When we take the time to express appreciation for the people and things in our life—what we have expands.

FYI: Oprah Winfrey often speaks about appreciation. Her grandmother, who raised her until she was six, gave her praise that she needed to cope with hardship in her later childhood and adolescence. She feels that this small amount of appreciation saved her life.

When we do not appreciate the people and things in our life, we find that they fade away.

Most Things We Desire Take Time to Achieve

Learning is accomplished through the exploration of knowledge followed by self-discovery. I'm passing along information that I've learned in my thirty years of work as a psychotherapist that you may want to consider. I am encouraging you to think for yourself. Changing negative patterns or beliefs takes time. Small steps are meaningful and they contribute to large changes over time. Patience is a virtue!

We Need To Care About the Needs, Feelings and Desires of Our Selves and Others

Caring about the needs, feelings and desires of yourself and others is called *kindness*. It requires an understanding that all living things have intrinsic value. Everyone can tune into his/her ability to create what they want in the world and assist others to do the same.

Creating "Win-Win" Situations Acknowledges Another's Point-of-View

Life should be a cooperative endeavor. By acknowledging that others have a right to their point of view, we can bridge forces of opposition and learn to mutually respect each other's perspective.

Your Need for Positive Self-Talk

Note:
We are what we believe. In order to change our circumstances, we need to:

- *Alter our beliefs*
- *Consciously stop projecting any unhealthy conditions into the future*
- *Stop assigning inappropriate power to past events.*

If you grew up in a negative household, it's very likely that the thoughts you hear in your head include a lot of "shoulds" and "can'ts."

Many people who grew up in a negative household adopt the language that they hear in their home. I had lunch in a restaurant the day I began thinking about this section and the man at the next table called his young son a pig when he missed his mouth and dropped food on his chin. That imprint might not sting if the boy's father provides enough praise to balance out his thoughtless remark but that little boy may end up in a therapist's office some day and say, "my father used to call me a pig."

Negative Programming

Negative programming is a powerful block to personal progress but it's really only a paper wall. My patients have varying abilities when it comes to punching through their paper walls. Some punch through their paper wall quickly and others take years to study and plan how to break through the paper.

Regardless of the programming that was embedded in your young subconscious mind, it's up to you to replace it.

Your Brain Believes What It Hears

Many of my patients have not punched through their paper wall because they're still holding on to negative programming from their parents:

"You'll never amount to anything."

"You're not smart."

"You're fat."

Patient: "I don't know why I feel so awful."
Guy: Let's talk about what you're saying to yourself."

Quote: "I paint objects as I think them, not as I see them."

- Pablo Picasso

"You're a slob."

"You're a loser."

By the time people arrive in my office the embedded programming has formed an endless loop of negative self-talk:

"I'm not smart."

"I hate myself."

"I'm a loser."

"I'll never be successful."

Wrestling With Your Subconscious

Note:

I've often made tapes for my patients and asked them to play them at home. I like to record positive affirmations with the sound of the sea or New Age music in the background. This extra dimension helps when you need to reach a meditative state. Although tapes are helpful in the background when you're on-the-go, meditation-style tapes help to clear clutter from your mind.

As adults, our beliefs about ourselves are very fixed. Should you decide that you need to re-program, you will need rigorous repetition or your subconscious will over-power whatever re-programming you try to do. Consider the following:

Step 1: Check for Negative Behavior Patterns

Check the Manfred Max-Neef Basic Human Needs chart to see if you have any of the negative behavior patterns listed in the "Negative Behavior When Needs Are Not Met" columns.

Step 2: Create a Card with Positive Self-Talk

Use a post-it note or an index card and create a positive statement that challenges one of your negative patterns. Refer to the chart in this section for help with this. Precede each of your positive statements with "I love myself" stated three times.

For example, if your self-esteem has been damaged (Subsistence), write the following statement on your card (in present tense):

"I am lovable, I am lovable, I am lovable and I'm feeling confident about my abilities."

Tape the card on the mirror in your bathroom or over the sink in your kitchen so that you'll see it every morning and evening.

Step 3: Create an Audio Tape with Positive Self-Talk

Your brain will need as much positive sensory input as possible. Consider purchasing a handheld audio tape recorder at an electronics store (approximately $30) and

Quote: "In creative visualization you use your imagination to create a clear image of something you wish to manifest. Then you continue to focus on the idea or picture regularly, giving it positive energy until it becomes objective reality...in other words, until you actually achieve what you have been visualizing."

- Shakti Gawain
Creative Visualization

make a tape of your self-talk. Fill the tape with 10 to 20 minutes of self-talk. Repeat your statement with a ten second break in-between recordings or add other positive self-talk statements. Take your recorder into the bathroom and play it as you get ready for work in the morning and as you get ready for bed in the evening.

Step 4: Look for Other Opportunities to Talk to Yourself

Your brain will need constant repetition to re-program the embedded data that's occupied your subconscious for decades. Look for other places to tape your index cards and take your recorder with you in the car.

With persistence, your new programming will begin to re-shape your beliefs. Your new beliefs will shape new attitudes, the attitudes will create new feelings, and eventually, your feelings will prompt new actions.

Step 5: Reinforce Positive Self-Talk with Imagery

Your positive self-talk will be even more effective if you create a visual movie in your mind that reinforces your positive statements. Visual imagery helps to program your mind—and your mind will believe that your images are real. Athletes who visualize physical skills actually develop "muscle memory" that help them engage in the real activity.

Positive Statements That Challenge Negative Self-Talk

As you get accustomed to positive self-talk, you will learn how important it is to create your own statements to challenge your embedded programming. If you're having trouble composing your own, the chart on the next page might help you get a jump start.

Manfred Max-Neef Basic Human Needs	Negative Behavior Pattern	Positive Statement
Subsistence	Damage to self-esteem. Overly cautious and fearful.	"I'm feeling confident about my abilities."
Protection	Does not trust. Never feels safe.	"I trust that I will take care of myself and make good decisions about people in my life."
Affection	Avoids intimacy, feels unworthy of love.	"I'm capable of giving love and I am worthy of receiving love. I will actively seek loving people to be around."
Understanding	Envious, jealous, has trouble expressing needs.	"I'm entitled to have my needs met. I'm worthy of love. I am in control of my fear."
Participation	Feels abandoned, isolated.	"People want a relationship with me. I can choose faithful, good, loving people to spend time with."
Idleness	Cannot relax.	"I'm entitled to have fun and to enjoy myself and others."

Manfred Max-Neef Basic Human Needs	Negative Behavior Pattern	Positive Statement
Creation	Not confident about talent or intelligence.	"I am an intelligent human being. I make good decisions and I learn from my mistakes."
Identity	Feels weak and passive, overly accommodating.	"I have deep inner strength. I'm entitled to my feeling. I'm entitled to express them."
Freedom	Angry, may feel controlled. Has no respect for authority. Overemphasis on work. May feel pressured to attain success.	"I am only controlled if I choose to be and I have the freedom to pursue my dreams at my pace."
Transcendence	Feels disillusioned.	"I'm strong enough to face reality—both good and bad."

Meet Anna

Note:
Anna's older brother and sister were the source of her early negative embedded programming. She did not make the connection until she had problems with her marriage.

In the context of couples marriage counseling, it is very common for my patients to trace their difficulties to events that occurred when they were children. Anna, age 36, came to see me in the first nine months that she was married. At our first meeting, I asked her about her problem:

> "My husband and I have been fighting for almost as long as we've been married. I'm afraid we'll break up. He's drinking excessively. We're in financial trouble and he may lose his business."

I repeated what I thought she was saying, "You're afraid for your marriage and husband's livelihood and you believe he's out of control."

> "Yes, the more he's out of control, the more I try to control him. It drives me crazy. I've had anxiety and depression problems all my life. I've seen several therapists and I've also taken medication for depression and obsessive compulsion. The worst part is—I feel unsure of myself. I feel very insecure and I also feel betrayed."

Jim came with Anna so I talked to both of them about their marriage. I asked each of them why they got married. Anna said,

> "Jim was so secure, I thought he would mellow out my moods and stabilize me. I thought he'd make me feel secure."

FYI: Anna's therapists treated her for depression and obsessive compulsion. Obsession is the intrusion of negative thoughts and compulsion is what you do to get rid of negative thoughts.

Jim said,

> "I married Anna because she said positive things about me. She seemed to adore me."

They both grimaced and said,

> "It looks like we're not fulfilling the reasons we got married."

I asked Jim if he felt he was out of control.

> "Yes, I could lose my business."

Jim's drinking problem is an addiction and I asked him to see a specialist. He agreed to make an appointment. When Anna heard that Jim was willing to see a counselor about his drinking, she seemed calmer. I asked her about this.

> "I do feel calmer. I was afraid he would be in denial."

Next, I asked Anna about her depression and feelings of insecurity.

> "I've been this way for as long as I can remember. I come from a good family. My parents were both well-educated. I had a nice life—we had an upper class lifestyle. I had an older brother and sister who made fun of me. They'd tell me I was dumb and stupid. Now that I think about it—they were brutal. They made me feel bad about myself. They ridiculed me. When we visited family friends, everyone ganged up on me. It seemed to be a sport."

FYI: Many experts believe that personality disorders are formed between the ages of 0 and 5 and that's why they're so hard to treat. Damage is done very early and it's ingrained.

I asked Anna how old she was when her family made fun of her.

> "I remember I was very young—probably between three and five years old. Even though my parents were loving, they forced me to go with them to their friend's house. They told me I was a baby when I complained. I remember my mother spanked me and told me to 'toughen up.' The ridicule left me feeling so insecure about everything. I'd even ask my sister if my Barbie doll looked right."

I told Anna that she did not deserve to be ridiculed at a young age and asked her if she ever trusts her gut.

> "No, I always question it."

We're Trained Not to Trust Our Gut

I explained to Anna that when we're small, we're very intuitive. If adults lie about what's happening, we believe them because they're adults. If this occurs, it trains us not to trust our gut.

> "That makes sense. A lot of people tell me to trust my intuition more than I do."

I told Anna that I suspected that her gut told her that Jim was drinking excessively and asked her when she started to have suspicions.

> "I felt suspicious about three months ago. I did not listen to my intuition. My mind kept telling me that Jim loves me and he wouldn't risk his job or our marriage."

Jim confirmed the fact that he had been drinking excessively for three months and I told Anna that she needed to learn to trust her intuition. Trusting her gut would help her with her anxiety and obsessions.

To reinforce the idea that Anna should trust her gut, I asked her to think about the times that she had made decisions that were mistakes.

"There have been five or six times."

I asked Anna to think about how her gut felt before she made the decisions.

"My gut was telling me not to—and my mind told me I would be able to work it out. I guess my gut was right."

I told Anna that we would need to work on self-talk statements that would reinforce her trust. Here are the statements that we created together:

"When I trust my gut, the decision is usually right."

"I'm a smart and intuitive woman and I can use my intuition to make good decisions."

To help Anna reprogram negative memories from her sister and brother, we talked about Anna's art ability. Here's a statement we created to reprogram Anna's childhood memory of her ability to dress her Barbie doll:

"I can dress my Barbie doll better than my sister because I am an artist."

Tip: To create a positive self-talk statement, simply create a phrase that is the opposite of the negative statements you hear in your head.

I asked Anna what type of artwork she did.

"I paint landscapes."

I asked Anna to bring her paintings into the office. I told her I thought that she was probably a very good painter because she loved her artwork.

"I will show you my paintings."

I told her I would look forward to seeing her artwork.

Challenging Anna's negative thinking is the key to unlocking her intuition. If she's an accomplished artist as an adult, then it is absurd that she was not creative enough to dress her Barbie doll when she was a child.

Perseverance Is the Key to Success

Anna will have to work hard to overcome the negative programming she received when she was young. She'll need to persevere—which is the key to overcoming any obstacle. Experts do say perseverence can be developed. The November 2005 issue of *Psychology Today* has a cover article called "The Winning Edge" that says achievement hinges on "grit" that author Peter Doskoch says is a mix of passion and perseverence.

Meet Lynn

Family systems therapy is fairly new. Shortly after World War II, therapists noticed intergenerational patterns. In a healthy family, each family member is allowed to have his or her sense of self and the family members provide emotional support to withstand any changes that occur. In contrast, dysfunctional families resist change and tension emerges whenever there are shifts.

Lynn is an example of a patient who created change in her family system when she decided to seek the help of a therapist. She had survived a harsh childhood with alcoholics and although she thought that a therapist would blame her for her family's dysfunction, she pushed herself to make an appointment to see me.

Therapists Can Help Challenge Patient Belief Systems

Patients often assume that a therapist will tell them what to do. When they arrive in counseling, they soon realize that they're the ones who must work on themselves and and try to see the world from new perspectives. Each person really does this for themselves. Therapists can help:

• Challenge a person's beliefs in a positive way

• Reshape a person's negative beliefs

• Help a person feel better about themselves

The relationship you form with your therapist should be based on trust. If you trust your therapist, they can act as a sounding board while you work on your beliefs.

The Patient Is Actually the Family System

Lynn reached an important milestone in therapy when she realized that the addiction problems in her family

FYI: In family systems therapy, people cannot be understood in isolation. They are influenced by their family of origin's rules, structure and organization.

caused rigid behavior patterns and communication blocks had become automatic. Her breakthrough came when she realized that she did not come from a healthy family that allowed members to have their own identity and maintain emotional connections to other members. She emerged from the family's dysfunction but the others resisted change.

Timing Is Critical

When Lynn first started therapy, she endured the feelings of shock and sadness that we described in the previous chapter. It took time for her positive self-talk to sink in. She mulled over positive ideas about herself between sessions until she was ready to accept them. She admits that her positive self-talk had to be repeated over and over. She uses the word "nuggets" to describe her positive self-talk:

> "I always walked away with at least one, what I like to call 'nugget' that would stay with me. I would think about it over and over, and feel a sense of peace—no pressure to think or act a certain way for someone else's benefit. The only one I needed to concentrate on was me."

Many years later, Lynn remembers several of her nuggets:

> "When I was trying to find love and was a bit promiscuous, Guy said, 'So you were a slut for a while, big deal!' He made me feel as though I was not a bad person and helped my guilt and shame disappear. When I was struggling to connect with my stepchildren, Guy

FYI: Family systems theory is an approach to therapy that emphasizes an interdependency among family members. Concepts include:

System - A family as an organism with internal rules, patterns of functioning and resistance to change. A person can best be understood in terms of their family system.

Rules - Family systems are governed by spoken and unspoken rules that influence communication, expression of feelings, privacy, gender roles and other forms of differentiation.

Roles - Every system includes roles (e.g., principal dysfunctional member, enabler, hero, rebel, clown and lost member). In healthy families, members exchange roles. Roles are acceptable if they help a person or situation but are detrimental if they block a person's growth. Roles become rigid when there is stress.

said, 'All you have to do is smile at them once in a while.' His comment took the pressure off immediately and I realized I was not being a bad parent. I released my guilt because I felt I was doing the best I could. And when I was struggling with my alcoholic husband, Guy said, 'He's sick and he's crazy.' His remark validated me and helped me realize that I was dealing with someone who was not rational, and I was fighting a battle that I was not going to win."

Seek Help From Someone Who Loves You

If you're not in therapy, enlist the help of someone who loves you—who can provide the type of support I've described. Create a Self-Talk Assistance Program (STAP) with someone who can help you form a different perspective:

Identify a Negative Thought That Is Causing Pain

Most people know what thoughts are causing pain. Flipping it or twisting it into a positive thought is usually the challenging part.

Ask for Assistance By Saying, "I Need Help"

Ask another party to help you reshape your negative thought. Many people will find that this step gets their creative juices flowing. Once you've created your self-talk statement, ask your friend or loved one to be a patient coach who non-judgmentally gives you permission to see things in an alternate way. Ask them to help you feel better about yourself—by behaving or talking as though your new thought pattern has already replaced the old.

FYI: Therapists who use family systems theory usually explore a person's family history to investigate behavior patterns. Behavior patterns can be influenced by a family's structure and boundaries and can be healthy or pathological:

Boundaries - Boundaries can protect privacy but can also limit the flow of information. In a healthy family, information passes from one person to another and inappropriate information is limited. In dysfunctional families, there may be blocks in communication and emotional exchanges. There may also be problems with privacy and individuation.

Enmeshment - In a dysfunctional, enmeshed family, it is difficult to distinguish between one person's emotions and another's.

Imbalanced Structure - In a dysfunctional family, children may have more power or responsibility than one or both parents.

Don't Stop

Realize that it is not easy to reprogram your beliefs about yourself. Even though you have enlisted the help of a coach, it is really you who will need to embrace change. It can be done, but the process often requires patience and perseverence.

Notes

Chapter 3

RULE #3

When You Consistently Under or Overreact Emotionally to People, Places or Things, It's Probably Transference

In the movies as in life, a person's backstory is everything that occurred in his/her past. In psychotherapy it's called their "family of origin."

"There's not a person on the planet who's not affected by negative and positive transference. It's the result of emotional imprinting, and each imprint carries repressed feelings that can be triggered when we encounter people, places or things that are similar. Although transference was mentioned in my training, and later in my practice, I learned that it's an extremely powerful concept.

Discovering transference issues in our lives provides us with an ability to break loose from psychological ties that bind us—and to use transference as a tool to navigate the world. In this chapter, we'll use an emotional scaling tool to zero in on any distortions that are triggering transference; we'll learn to consciously identify painful emotional imprints; and then we'll learn to train the psyche to get comfortable with similar imprints that are experienced as an adult."

Learning About Transference

The human brain is constantly being programmed by life experiences—both positive and negative. If you grew up around a group of dysfunctional people, think carefully about who you turned to for some healthy programming. He or she helped embed memories that you can now nurture and grow to gradually replace the negative dysfunctional set of data.

Transference Occurs as Emotional Triggers

Throughout our lives, the positive and negative memories that are stored in our brains form connections to new life experiences. Although this happens every day, most people do not notice that it takes place. As we make these connections, there are emotional feelings that are triggered at the same time. If the emotion that is stored is powerful—it may cause us to make an unrealistic assumption about the new life experience. Numerous possibilities exist:

Situation	Older Memory	Present Feeling
Gary, age 28, briefly meets the tenant next door.	**Negative:** Gary was abused by his mother.	**Negative Transference:** Gary is unsure about why he does not like his neighbor. Later, he realized she looks like his mother.
Carol, age 30, accepts a job and her boss is Japanese.	**Positive:** Carol had a previous boss who was Japanese and was very kind.	**Positive Transference:** Carol's earlier positive experience makes her feel super-enthusiastic about her new job.

Situation	Older Memory	Present Feeling
Emily, age 27, moves in with Jennifer, a roommate who has a very clean apartment.	**Negative:** When Emily was a young child, her mother went into a rage when she felt a family member had left something out of place.	**Negative Transference:** Emily feels anxious and on-edge if she does not keep the apartment clean.
Paul, age 30, begins dating a woman who loves classical music.	**Positive:** Paul's grandfather loved classical music and spent a lot of time teaching Paul about classical composers.	**Positive Transference:** Every time Paul and his new girlfriend listen to classical music, the experience triggers wonderful memories and endears him to his girlfriend.
Charles, age 28, begins dating a woman who uses shame to get him to do what she wants.	**Negative:** Charles' parents both used shame to manipulate him.	**Negative Transference:** Charles is accustomed to people who use shame to manipulate him. He feels like an insecure child when he's with his girlfriend and he's vulnerable to her manipulation. *Note:* Charles is an example of someone who is stuck in a dynamic with another person because it is *familiar.*

Situation	Older Memory	Present Feeling
Angela's new boyfriend drinks excessively and it ruins the time they spend together.	**Positive:** Angela's parents drank responsibly.	**Positive Transference:** Angela realizes that her boyfriend has a problem that requires more help than she can provide. She decides to set a boundary in their relationship. She will go to Al-Anon and he must successfully go through treatment for his alcohol or she will break off the relationship. *Note:* In this case, Angela's parents were good role models and she learned an appropriate response.
John's new girlfriend showers him with attention, wants to be with him constantly and gets upset when he leaves.	**Negative:** John's father was overly protective of his mother and did not like her to go anywhere without him.	**Negative Transference:** John likes the attention from his girlfriend and he is blinded concerning his girlfriend's emotional immaturity and later feels very smothered.

Quote: "Everybody should do at least two things each day that he hates to do, just for practice."

- William James
  Philosopher

The amount of transference we experience depends on the strength of the associated emotion that is stored in our memory. Childhood memories are usually connected to powerful emotions. Remember the concept of valence in science class? A positive or negative charge with a strong valence can overpower a weaker, opposite charge and valence values with the same type of charge will have an additive effect. In other words, two negatives will add up to a greater negative and two positives will add up to a greater positive.

Deja vous?

FYI: It is a common mistake for codependents to say, "I'll take you back if you go to counseling." People who are involved with alcoholics need a much stronger set of conditions. Instead of agreeing to take an alcoholic back, the codependent should say, "We will talk about getting back together when:

• you're going to AA on a regular basis

• you have completed treatment

• I have a positive conversation with your AA sponsor

• I have a positive conversation with your therapist"

Transference Often Goes Unnoticed

As you can imagine, transference causes friction in relationships. Unfortunately, most people have never heard of transference. To locate or identify transference, it's necessary to analyze the emotions that have been stored in our memory banks. The next section contains a data collection exercise that I use to help a patient scan his/her emotional imprints. Because transference is dependent on the strength of a stored emotion, you will be required to use a number scale and assign a value to your stored emotions.

Identifying Transference

Note:
Everyone's situation is unique—you're the one who will need to analyze your family system. To do this, you will need to collect data and zero in on the feeling.

When I started working on this chapter, I wanted to develop a self-help exercise for readers to identify transference issues that may have their roots in early family experiences. The exercise I had created contained questions that are similar to the questions I use in counseling sessions. Because transference can touch so many life experiences, I soon realized that the list of questions was far too long for this chapter.

Instead of asking the reader to answer questions, I will describe the process I use to uncover transference in my patients using the case studies presented in this book. In this way, readers will be able to learn by example.

The Transference Tree

I use an image of a tree to help me organize a patient's history. A tree provides a map or template to a person's issues that might trigger transference. What's important to understand is that the tree will only contain issues that carry a strong negative or a strong positive feeling. The feelings in between are considered neutral and do not trigger transference.

Tree	Template Element
Roots	Roots correspond to a person's family of origin and their early childhood experiences.
Trunk	In our template, the trunk's pathways are a person's positive and negative life

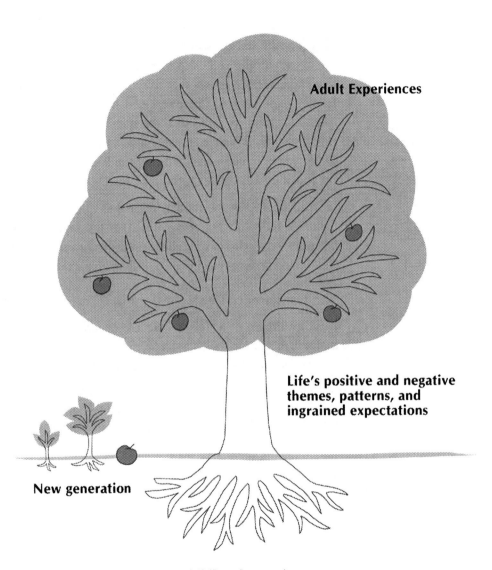

Adult Experiences

Life's positive and negative themes, patterns, and ingrained expectations

New generation

Childhood Experiences

Transference tree

Quote: "A [person] is ethical only when life, as such, is sacred to him, that of plants and animals as that of his fellow men, and when he devotes himself hopefully to all life that is in need of help."

- Albert Schweitzer

Tree	Template Element
Trunk (continued)	themes. Examples include codependency, abandonment, self-worth, mistrust, guilt, rigid standards. Themes are usually connected to pain from childhood. They're also patterns that become repetitious if we don't work on them.
Branches and Leaves	The tree's upper anatomy corresponds to adult experiences. Any seeds or fruit produced by the tree correspond to children. As the seeds or fruit with seeds fall, a new tree grows nearby representing the start of a forest—a dysfunctional forest.

Transference Is Pervasive

The chart in the next section contains a summary of how transference plays a part in each of the patient cases presented in this book. The chart provides a preview of their case histories. Also included are the person's life themes and the resolution. Because psychotherapy is learned by studying people and their case histories, you may want to use the chart as a resource for reviewing the concepts covered in this book.

Patient/Chapter/Topic	Childhood Experiences With a Strong + - Charge	Adult Experiences With a Strong + - Charge
Marilyn Chapter One Childhood Roles	**Negative:** Alcoholic Father Codependent Mother Hero child who had to take care of her two younger brothers. **Positive:** She learned how to be innovative and work hard.	**Negative:** Married a self-centered alcoholic Takes care of everyone wherever she goes **Positive:** Developed good managerial skills and earned a good living.
Anna Chapter Two Positive Self-Talk	**Negative:** Older brother and sister ridiculed her. **Positive:** Artistic and explored this talent as a child.	**Negative:** Problem with depression, feelings of insecurity and obsessive compulsive behavior. **Positive:** Creative as an adult, works as a makeup artist.
Bruce Chapter Three Transference	**Negative:** Mother is a perfectionist who used shame, guilt and rejection to control him. **Positive:** He learned how to work hard and "do it right the first time." He was extremely likeable.	**Negative:** Driven by unrelenting standards due to feelings of inadequacy. He's a magnet for women with problems (emotionally and financially strapped women who never get better) **Positive:** Climbed ranks in the military and business. Takes care of women.

Life Themes	Possible Transference Issues	Resolution
• If I take care of everyone before myself—I'll be OK. • I'm not worthy unless I work hard. • The people around me are never OK. • Men are more important than women. • There are no such thing as boundaries.	Marilyn is most vulnerable to transference in her relationships with men and possibly her own children since she learned to be a caretaker. People are attracted to partners whose behavior is familiar and Marilyn will need to avoid self-centered men with problems.	Marilyn needs to use her innovative talents for herself, set boundaries, work on building a positive self-image using positive self-talk and learn that a positive self-image is not dependent on helping.
• I am "too..." (too dumb, too insecure, too anxious).	Anna needs to watch for transference issues in situations with authority figures.	Anna needs to trust her gut and assert herself. She also needs to challenge authority and practice using positive self-talk.
• I'm not perfect enough, I can do better. • I'm a sinful individual who needs to make amends. • If I can help her to be OK, then I'll be lovable.	Bruce would be vulnerable to transference issues in any relationship where someone tries to manipulate him with guilt and shame.	Bruce needs to feel positive about himself or to have mercy on himself and feel like he's worthy of a woman who's together. He also needs to feel that he's human and fallible (like the rest of us).

Patient/Chapter/Topic	Childhood Experiences With a Strong + - Charge	Adult Experiences With a Strong + - Charge
Laura Chapter Four Codependency	**Negative:** Mother is an alcoholic/narcissist who mercilessly harrassed Laura about her weight. **Positive:** Very smart and social in school; did well academically and developed lasting friendships.	**Negative:** First husband was a wife-beater and second husband is an alcoholic. Codependently takes care of people at work and at home. **Positive:** Very social as an adult and is an excellent manager at work. Her meaningful friendships have provided a valuable support system.
Jerry (Introvert) Chapter Five Personality Types	**Negative:** Flooded by athletic coaches as a child. **Positive:** Very thoughtful and loyal (like many introverts).	**Negative:** Flooded by coworkers as an adult. **Positive:** Learned that introverts drain around people—especially extroverts who flood.
Jim (Jim and Carrie) Chapter Six First Contracts in Marriage	**Negative:** Extreme childhood abuse and neglect. **Positive:** Smart, learned to do things right the first time so he would not get punished.	**Negative:** Feelings of negative self-worth followed him into adulthood. Fearful of any type of abuse (hypervigilant) **Positive:** Married someone who would take care of him.

Themes	Possible Transference Issues	Resolution
• I'm not OK because I'm fat. • I need to take second best because I'm heavy. • The only way I can feel good about myself is to take care of others. • If I can take care of people, they will change and then they will take care of me.	Laura married two narcissistic males who used her. She codependently takes care of everyone.	Laura's supportive friends have helped her resolve her issues. She set boundaries and disowned most of her family—keeping the positive ones who do not drain her. She's learning to take care of herself.
• I'm odd and strange because I'm introverted.	Learned to duck people who were similar to his childhood coaches.	Learned strategies for dealing with extroverts.
• If I speak up, someone will hit me and hurt me. • I'm not good enough because I do things wrong. • I'm smart but forgetful. • I have to finish every project within the same day or weekend and it needs to be perfect.	Because of his childhood experiences, Jim learned to be either avoidant or aggressive.	Jim needs to realistically evaluate his relationship with his wife and not see her as a monster. He also needs to learn to be assertive rather than aggressive.

Patient/Chapter/Topic	Childhood Experiences With a Strong + - Charge	Adult Experiences With a Strong + - Charge
Jason Chapter Seven Communication Tools	**Negative:** Father was physically and mentally abusive. Witnessed his father beating his mother. **Positive:** Survived childhood.	**Negative:** Explosive temper. Arrested for throwing a picture through a window. **Positive:** Successful, hard worker.
Josh Chapter Eight Control/Enmeshment	**Negative:** Lost his mother and father very early. **Positive:** Had a nice step-father.	**Negative:** Stole hip-hop jewelry that gave him prestige with his peers. **Positive:** Good musically.
Richard Chapter Nine Good Growth Follows Bad	**Negative:** Overweight as a child. Classmates made cruel comments. **Positive:** Very supportive parents. Grew up feeling that there were people who loved him.	**Negative:** Married a trophy wife who left him for another man. **Positive:** Smart and has talent as a cook.
Carla Chapter Ten Intuition	**Negative:** Father and mother were extremely controlling. **Positive:** Followed rules, good in school.	**Negative:** Married son of father's best friend even though her gut told her not to. **Positive:** Bright, very good with people.

Themes	Possible Transference Issues	Resolution
• Life is war. • You're not a man if you're afraid.	Jason is insecure and afraid like his father. He covers it up with anger.	When Jason feels fear, he needs to identify the feeling and work on responding with assertiveness rather than aggression. Positive self-talk will also help him to develop empathy.
• I'm not good enough, smart enough or worthy enough.	Josh felt abandoned and grew up not trusting adults.	Getting him to talk about his abandonment and trust issues helped him with his self-concept (Note: See the details of Josh's "deal" in Chapter 8).
• I'm not good enough, because I'm fat. • If I can hook up with a babe, I won't be an insecure fat kid.	Richard felt like an insecure fat kid all of the time. He covered it up by marrying a shallow babe.	Through divorce, Richard discovered good things about himself. Through positive self-talk, he feels OK even though he's overweight. He also found someone who loves him.
• If I'm good enough, I'll get what I want. • God will get you if you don't do what your parents tell you to do.	Carla's fear of authority caused her to disown her own needs.	Carla needs to learn to trust her gut, assert herself and challenge authority. Positive self-talk will help her develop a positive self-image.

Patient/Chapter/Topic	Childhood Experiences With a Strong + - Charge	Adult Experiences With a Strong + - Charge
Carol Chapter Eleven Denial	**Negative:** Had a very strict and self-centered father. Very heavy and unattractive until she was seventeen. **Positive:** Did well in school and has good female friends.	**Negative:** Feels unattractive even though she is good-looking. **Positive:** Has a good job and is very bright intellectually.
June Chapter Twelve Predictive Behavior	**Negative:** Passive because of mother's extreme control. Weak ego strength, did not develop a strong sense of self. **Positive:** Well taken care of, followed rules, did well in school.	**Negative:** Vulnerable to authoritarian men. Struggles with confrontation. **Positive:** Competent at work, good with bosses.
Chapter Thirteen Personality Disorders	Note: Personality-disordered people don't/can't change.	

Themes	Possible Transference Issues	Resolution
• I'm not good enough. • I can never please my father.	Father's behavior leaves her vulnerable to authoritarian men who complement her.	Takes a good look at herself and learns that she is an attractive human being physically and emotionally. She also learns to trust her gut concerning what's good for her.
• I'm responsible for my mother and for everyone. • I'm not competent to be on my own. • Other peoples' opinions are better than mine. • It's hard for me to talk to people.	May marry an authoritarian male. She may also overwork to please her boss. It's hard for her to set clear boundaries because of her codependency.	Needs to: • work on assertiveness • practice confrontation • put her own needs before or equal to others • accept her positive abilities and talk about them • set clear boundaries— especially with people close to her

Quote: "Women now have choices. They can be married, not married, have a job, not have a job, be married with children, unmarried with children. Men have the same choice we've always had: work, or prison."

- Tim Allen
  Comedian

"Remember, he's not like your father, your brother or your previous boyfriend. He's a a nice guy."

Connecting the Past and the Present

Note:
I frequently tell my patients that a relationship is like a dance. Two people learn the steps and can anticipate each other's moves. Neither partner can change the other's steps—only his/her own. When one of the partners decides to change his/her steps, they will both need to change—or stop dancing.

A critical point in resolving a transference issue occurs when you identify a painful emotional imprint in your childhood and connect it to an unrealistic emotional reaction in the present.

As adults, we're able to gain control of our emotions far better than we did as children. Adults who see their transference connections can not only gain control of their emotions, but they can also work on embedding newer, positive memories over old tracks.

Strategies for Conquering Transference

Living with others is often hard. If transference is causing friction in one or more of your relationships, the steps for conquering transference include:

- Understanding transference

- Re-programming your thinking if transference is causing a problem

- Setting clear boundaries in your relationships where you have identified transference. Boundaries are limits and they're considered to be a healthy element. We'll explore this topic in more depth in the next chapter.

Create Positive Self-Talk Statements

If transference is causing stress in your relationship, it is up to you to work on your own steps. Once you're clear about your triggers, use the steps provided in the previous chapter to create positive self-talk statements to reprogram your subconscious. Here are some additional strategies to help you with your positive self-talk:

- Appreciate this positive image and know that it will expand (Note: What you appreciate expands and what you do not appreciate fades away).

- Put the negative experience in a quieter place so that it does not influence the present.

- Do not project your negative experience into the future.

Re-programming: Replacing Negative Self-Talk

Four of the adults in the Learning About Transference section have negative feelings due to their older memories. The following chart recaps each of their situations and provides an example of a positive statement they can use to replace their negative self-talk:

Patient/Present Situation	Positive Statement	Possible Next Step
Gary Gary's next-door neighbor resembles his mother who abused him.	"She's not my mother and my experience with my neighbor has been very positive. Not everyone who looks like my mother is abusive."	Gary will make an effort to be friendly to his neighbor unless she gives him a reason not to be.
Emily Emily's new roommate is very clean and her habits remind Emily of her mother, who was often enraged when something was not clean or was out of-place.	"My mother was extreme; my roommate is just clean and that's OK. My roommate is not my mother."	Emily might tell her roommate her history, which may help her to understand if Emily occasionally over-reacts.

Patient/Present Situation	Positive Statement	Possible Next Step
Charles Charles has been dating a woman who uses shame to get him to do what she wants.	"I'm an adult and I know what's right. I know what I want and what I don't want. I will make decisions based on my needs (as opposed to shaming). If someone is shaming me, I will do the opposite." *Note:* Codependent heroes are usually sensitive to shame, and I will often tell them to do the opposite of what the shaming person tells them to do.	Charles might sit down with his girlfriend and explain how she has been shaming him. By doing this, Charles is challenging what has been done to him and giving notice that he is setting boundaries.
John John's new girlfriend showers him with attention but she's emotionally immature and gets upset when he leaves. John's father was overprotective of his mother and now John is feeling stifled by his girlfriend's behavior. He is also confused about what is normal.	"I'm an adult and I'm OK with myself. My father was overprotective of my mother and taught me to be vulnerable to overly dependent women. I'm OK the way that I am. I don't need to be showered with attention all the time."	John might sit down with his girlfriend and talk about what's going on. He might also ask her to work on becoming independent (a contract). John will need to decide how much patience he has concerning her progress. If the agreement does not work, he may need to leave the relationship.

Meet Bruce

Bruce is a Vietnam veteran who is not unlike today's wounded veterans who have asked to be sent back to the war zone even though they are physically disabled. Emotionally, they are heroes who want to do more. Although Bruce was not seriously wounded in Vietnam, he worked as a radio operator in his platoon and witnessed some of the worst carnage of the war. For years, he's been plagued with survivor guilt that is similar to the handicapped GIs who have asked to be sent back to Iraq.

Although it is admirable for someone to exhibit hero qualities, it's unhealthy for anyone to be stuck in this role and never exhibit any characteristics of life's opposite role—which in this case is a rebel.

Tapping Your Rebel is Healthy

In Chapter 1, we met Alice, whose predominant childhood role was a hero, and we learned how she tapped the rebel part of her personality when her dysfunctional mother neglected to pay her tuition.

Bruce's hero child emerged because of an entirely different set of circumstances. All of the adults in Alice's life drank and were irresponsible. In contrast, Bruce grew up on a dairy farm, which had a rigorous routine. His mother was a perfectionist who shamed him into doing everything right the first time. His do-it-right work ethic has made him shine all his life. Bruce was promoted in the military and throughout his career.

Bruce's transference issues surrounding the shame his mother used and the repetitious drill related to his parents' standards of perfection, set him up for an extraordinary amount of guilt. In referring to his experience in Vietnam,

FYI: Bruce's story is recorded in a book entitled *Lima-6: A Marine Company Commander in Vietnam*. It's a memoir written by retired Marine Colonel Richard S. Camp, who provides a very compelling account of the physical hardships and dangers encountered by young American soldiers who were only 18 and 19 years old.

Bruce frequently says, "I could have and should have done more." His dilemma is that it's impossible to be a perfectionist during a war. There's no way to "do it right the first time." If you survive—you've done it right.

Unlike Alice, who occasionally tapped the rebel part of her personality as a child, Bruce never really tapped his until recently.

Bruce was drafted and as a child of a strict family, dodging the draft was unthinkable. Instead, he did the right thing and went to Vietnam—a decision that had a huge price attached.

Bruce's Negative Transference

The shame that Bruce's mother used to manipulate him when he was a child has had a lasting negative effect on his relationships with women. Unknowingly, Bruce's mother created a hero who never questioned authority. As a result of the shaming tactic that his mother used to get him to do what she wanted, he attracts women who often use shame to manipulate him. He's accepted this behavior from women because it's familiar.

The role balancing I described in Chapter 1 is the solution for anyone who is stuck in their childhood role. Bruce is stuck in the role of a hero and he's gradually experimenting with life's opposite—which is the rebel.

It's been hard for Bruce to assess his transference issue that is related to his mother because she was a very good parent in many ways. He's ambivalent on whether his mother abused him. On the one hand, she was a good provider, his home had a lot of good structure and he felt

FYI: Another book, titled *Ambush Valley*, also provides a close-up look at Bruce's experience in Vietnam. Publisher's Weekly has called author Eric Hammel's work a "superb oral history." He describes one of the worst battles of the war that took place on September 7, 1967. On that date, Bruce's battalion moved into the DMZ and did not know that a Vietnamese regiment with twice the number of troops was close by. In two battles, the battalion lost over 40 percent of its men and the survivors barely escaped with their lives.

loved even though his parents were not demonstrative. In spite of this, his mother used shame to control him. Once we are able to understand that the traps we encounter as adults are rooted in our childhood, we can begin to make healthier decisions.

The Stockholm Syndrome

Bruce's recovery from the manipulation in his youth may be complicated by the fact that obedient, good kids often find it more difficult to survive extremely difficult situations than strong-willed, rebellious kids. A complication is the bonding that takes place between a victim and an abuser if the victim has low self-esteem. Bonding with an abuser is considered to be a victim survival strategy. Those with a strong need to please authority figures may be vulnerable to what has been called the *Stockholm Syndrome*— an expression first used in the early 70s to explain the behavior of hostages who identified with their captors. In Stockholm, Sweden in 1973, two machine-gun-carrying bank robbers held four hostages in a bank vault for six days. The incident received widespread notoriety because of the bonding that took place. In media interviews after their release, it became clear that the hostages supported their captors. One of the hostages became engaged to one of the criminals and another started a legal defense fund to help them with their criminal defense fees.

The *Stockholm Syndrome* is also commonly found in family and romantic relationships. Abusers can be fathers, mothers, husbands, wives, boyfriends or girlfriends, or any other person who is in a position of control or authority.

Quote: "Put yourself in a state of mind where you say to yourself, 'Here is an opportunity for me to celebrate like never before, my own power, my own ability to get myself to do whatever is necessary.'"

- Martin Luther King, Jr.

Whether or not someone has ever been a hostage is not the issue—it's the cluster of symptoms that is sometimes observed in people who have been abused, including:

• caring for an abuser

• bonding with an abuser

• seeking approval from an abuser

• depending on an abuser for security

• loss of identify in order to identify with an abuser

All children, teens and young adults need to develop the strength of character that's needed to survive adversity. Powerful well-meaning parents who feel the need to protect and micromanage may actually block circumstances that help young people learn how to survive. Similarly, if a family's circumstances causes a young person to become preoccupied with the needs of an authority figure, there's no room left for that person to develop a strong sense of their own identity.

Like a lot of heroes, Bruce was conditioned to take care of others. This may have also been due, in part, to the hero's need to maintain stability and avoid "trouble." In an abusive relationship where there are threats or any kind of verbal abuse, the victims may work overtime to control an external environment. Heroes are particularly good at anticipating every move, every topic and every issue that might trigger abuse. Unfortunately, this type of dynamic also causes the victim to experience a loss of self-esteem. In Bruce's case, he grew into an adult who was stuck in the role of taking care of others—leaving him open to the manipulations of both men and women who saw this trait in him. Once Bruce became involved with a manipulative woman, his tendency as a hero made him stay in the relationship.

Moving Out of Shaming Relationships

Bruce's history with women shows a repetitive pattern that is very common in people who have been abused. The shaming that his mother used to manipulate him in his youth left him vulnerable to women who used a similar form of manipulation. He married a woman who shamed him and then later lived with a woman who also shamed him. The shame that both women used is typical of people who see a need to manipulate others to survive. In the aftermath of a dysfunctional childhood, it is very common for an adult to exhibit one of two behavior patterns:

- Predator - Someone who is a predator is often an abuse victim. If abused in their childhood, there's no role model to learn from and predatory behavior becomes a survival mechanism. Predators may also have a personality disorder described in the last chapter.

- Victim - It is very common for an abused person to feel ashamed, responsible or guilty.

As an abuse survivor, Bruce was a hero/victim in relationships with other abuse survivors who drank and took advantage of him. The work Bruce did in therapy helped him identify his repetitive behavior patterns and work on change.

Quote: "War is fear cloaked in courage."

- William Westmoreland
  American General

Bruce's Beautiful Colleague Who Helped Him

A turning point occurred when he developed a platonic friendship with a woman doctor at work. She never shamed him, he liked her and they developed a very caring friendship. Even though they never became romantically involved, that relationship was the key to his therapeutic progress—a bridge to new, meaningful relationships with women who don't use shame to manipulate him. He finally broke his habitual pattern with women he needed to take care of and realized what it was like to be in a relationship with a competent friend who did not want anything from him.

Quote: "I did get a purple heart, but it was just for minor scratches. I think every one deserves one for the deep emotional scars and wounds on the inside. I'm not sure they will ever heal completely."

- Bruce

"Vietnam is a hell of a place to grow up."

Chapter 4

RULE #4

Codependency Is the Illusion That You Can Control or Fix Someone Else

"When a codependent dies, the life of their significant other flashes before their eyes."

- Timmen Cermak

"Long before I became a psychotherapist, I met people who truly believed their happiness was tied to another person's happiness. They consistently sacrificed their own needs for another person's. Although many were smart, and often successful, they were totally disconnected from their own needs and had no sense of self. Today, I realize that these people are codependents."

Learning About Codependency

Note:
Codependents have a distorted view of needs and wants. A need is related to survival and an example is the need for food. Wants are much less critical to survival but they're important for happiness and growth. If you have low self-esteem, it's very likely you'll consider your needs to be unimportant—particularly if you're a codependent who puts others' needs and wants ahead of your own.

In the 1970s, counselors who were treating alcoholics noticed that their patients often had spouses who had psychological struggles with the problems of their alcoholic partners. These partners were often consumed with the job of trying to fix or rescue the alcoholic. The term *codependent* was used to refer to a "co-alcoholic" whose rescuing role provided a sense of identity and distraction from his/her own fears and problems.

By the 1980s, counselors began to treat other addictions besides alcohol. As the disease of addiction was extended to cocaine, work, sex and gambling, the label of codependent was applied to those who exhibited the following characteristics:

Extreme Dependence on People or Things

Codependents are often afraid of being abandoned, ignored or shamed. They adapt to others' desires and in the process, they lose touch with their own wishes and needs.

Loss of Personal Identity

Codependents are so focused on pleasing or helping others that they disconnect from their own inner emotional life. When emotions surface, they are often painful, including feelings of loneliness, fear, shame and anger. The boundaries that set codependents apart from other people are blurred and codependents often feel responsible for the actions of others.

Quote: "Becoming a true adult is not a linear process. It will take you upward, downward, forward, backward and inside out. Expect to falter; expect to make mistakes. You will never be totally free of anxiety, fear, guilt, and confusion. No one is. But those demons will no longer control you. That is the key."

- Susan Forward, Ph.D.
  Toxic Parents

Need for Control

In their effort to take responsibility for others, codependents often expend energy trying to change other people. On the surface, they appear to be accommodating, but internally, they often resent their significant other for their unhappiness.

Lack of Respect in Personal Relationships

John Bradshaw, author of several books on codependency, describes the codependent as a person who is "out of touch with their feelings, needs and desires." Having no self-worth of their own, a codependent has "*others-worth*." Inside, they struggle with respect for themselves and often lack respect for their partner.

Forced Emotional Sacrifice

Codependent children are not whole people emotionally because circumstances forced them to cover for a family member in order to keep peace. In the process, they lost touch with their own needs, desires, thoughts and feelings.

Quote: "Let us now set forth one of the fundamental truths about marriage: the wife is in charge."

- Bill Cosby
  Comedian

Meet Laura

Note:

Codependents have a negative inner critic inside of their head that runs negative mantras that are related to childhood punishment, shame and guilt. By the time a codependent is an adult, this inner critic has a nasty, moralistic and forbidding voice.

Codependents usually struggle with self-esteem issues. An example is Laura, who came to see me on and off for a period of 15 years. Now, in her second marriage, Laura is suffering from anxiety disorder. Her first husband beat her and her second husband drinks. At the time of this writing, they are both losing their jobs and Laura recently tried to commit suicide by taking an overdose of pills. On the night she wanted to die, her husband found her unconscious and called an ambulance. While she was in intensive care, Laura told her mother what had happened and her mother disowned her. Laura's mother is an alcoholic and a narcissist—a very self-centered person who predictably placed all of the blame on Laura.

Laura was very heavy as a child, which was the cause of her low self-esteem. Her mother constantly belittled her, leaving Laura with feelings of low self-importance.

Codependents who don't have supportive families have a very hard time. Laura stayed with her second husband because he stopped drinking. They're working on their relationship and Laura is much more detached from family members who betrayed her when she needed help. She's living with the fact that her mother is self-centered and she's learning to care about herself instead of everyone else. She understands how important it is to consider her own needs rather than everyone else's.

Each of us is responsible for his/her own happiness. Trouble arises when you make others' health and happiness a top priority instead of *your own,* or when you expect others to put your health and happiness ahead of

Quote: "In its broadest sense, codependency can be defined as an addiction to people, behaviors or things. Codependency is the fallacy of trying to control interior feelings by controlling people, things and events on the outside."

- Dr. Robert Hemfelt, et al. *Love is a Choice*

their own. The result is codependency. When Laura began to learn about boundaries and set limits on what she did for others, she created a necessary *balance* in her life.

"You can either go to the family reunion or lose your inheritance—you choose."

Tools For Understanding Codependency

Note:
Our beliefs about ourselves shape our behavior. Often our beliefs are directly related to our need for approval—from parents, siblings and peers. If this need is not met, our self-esteem will suffer, and we may develop codependent behavior.

In chapter one, we looked at extremes to help understand the various roles in dysfunctional families. Similarly, let's look at behavior in people who exhibit:

- Extreme codependency
- Some codependency
- Very little codependency

Tool1: Behavior Continuum

Take a look at the following behavior continuum and try to think of people you know who fit into the range of behavior.

Extreme Codependency	Some Codependent Behavior	Little or No Codependency
Extreme codependents are drawn to occupations such as nursing and emergency care. This person is an "enabler" and they prefer to focus on—or control—other people at work and at home. Extreme codependents are often in marriages with a narcissist (Note: narcissism is covered in the final chapter).	This group is drawn to caretaking professions but they have healthy boundaries in their personal lives.	A person with little or no codependency is assertive rather than passive. He/she understands the meaning of the words "sovereign" and "individual." They are empathetic rather than sympathetic and they maintain healthy boundaries at work and at home.

Quote: "The ghosts of our past—our nurturing years and the childhoods of our parents and their parents on back—wrap their eerie fingers around our present."

- Dr. Robert Hemfelt, et al.
  Love is a Choice

Tool 2: Codependent Profiles

The following profiles describe people who have codependent behavior. Each of these people can choose to make changes or continue in their codependent circumstances. Read each of the profiles to determine if you understand which of their choices (a or b) is the codependent choice.

John

John is a middle-income high school teacher whose wife has spent all of their savings. Her addiction is ruining their marriage. She has a part-time job at a retail clothing store but she spends more than she makes. His wife hid the truth about her spending for a long time because she paid the bills. John can:

a. Choose not to deal with his wife directly but work on their financial problems. He can take a second job and borrow money to pay creditors who call his home.

b. Confront his wife and get a verbal commitment concerning a budget. He can also take over the job of paying the bills and stop borrowing money to pay his wife's debt.

Tom

Tom is a father of three grown children who all live with him. None of his children work, and they are constantly getting into trouble. His unmarried daughter who lives with him also has a young child. Tom can:

a. Continue to support his children and allow their problems to take over his life.

FYI: *Saturday Night Live*'s Al Franken wrote and starred in a film that's helpful for learning how to spot codependent behavior. It's called *Stuart Saves His Family*. The Stuart Smalley character (Al Franken) has a dysfunctional family that is almost a textbook case. Stuart is the peacemaker in the family and when an aunt dies, he is forced to confront his alcoholic father (actor Harris Yulin); his codependent enabler mother (actress Shirley Knight); his pot-smoking unemployed brother (actor Vincent D'Onofrio) and his overeater and thrice- divorced sister (actress Lesley Boone).

b. Create a timeline for his children to leave, including a plan for his daughter to leave her young child with him if she cannot support herself and her child.

Bruce

Bruce is a middle manager at a large manufacturing plant and he supervises a 12-person department. He fails to delegate work and he allows his department staff to walk all over him. The people he manages show up late for work and they know Bruce will cover for them when they do not complete their work. Bruce can:

a. Continue to allow his employees to walk over him and struggle with the work that piles up.

b. Delegate work to his employees and explain his expectations concerning their performance. When they fail to take responsibility for their actions, he can fire the most offensive member of his department as an example to the other staff.

Mary

Mary is an editor at a large publishing company that is famous for having a mean spirit. Employees do not say hello to each other and they sabotage each others' work. Mary recently discovered that everyone in her department has nightmares about their job and she realizes that the company has attracted people who come from abusive homes. She also feels that their low self-esteem prevents them from leaving their job. Mary has a decision to make. She can:

a.   Convince herself that it will be very hard to find another job and stay at the publishing company.

b.   Begin to look for another job, take night courses to acquire skills for finding a better job or quit her job and trust that she will find another job that she likes.

Barbara

Barbara is a veterinarian who is single. The man she has been dating has had trouble finding work for the past year and he's been living with her for six months. In that time, she has paid for nearly all of his expenses including his health insurance and car payments. Barbara is at a crossroads. She can:

a.   Continue to support her boyfriend and not confront him.

b.   Talk to him about their life together and ask him to create a timeline for finding work.

Strategies for Conquering Codependency

Note:
Recovery from codependency requires learning about detachment and boundaries

Codependents are people who devote their lives to saving others, but it's caring to an excess. Excessive caring becomes fixing and the codependent often becomes angry, controlling, blaming and manipulative:

"I'm not feeling good about myself now, but I will when I fix you."

The fixers are attracted to people who need a lot of help—alcoholics, drug addicts, con artists, criminals or possibly very troubled people who come from highly dysfunctional homes. If you suspect that you're codependent, the steps for recovery include:

- Understanding codependence

- Re-programming your thinking if codependence is causing a problem

- Setting clear boundaries in your relationships where you have identified codependence.

Taking Back Your Integrity

If you are a codependent and you're overly involved with someone who has a lot of personal problems, you need to take back your integrity. The dictionary defines integrity as the state of being complete or whole. The more integrity we have, the easier it is to set up boundaries. Codependents do not feel whole because they do not feel good about themselves. Once they learn that their happiness is not dependent on what anyone else does or thinks, they will break the codependent habit and begin to live life!

Quote: "At least one out of four children of alcoholic parents become alcoholics themselves, and many of these adults were given their first drink at a very young age by their parents."

- Susan Forward, Ph.D.
  Toxic Parents

Life Provides Us With Lessons

Once we accept that life is about lessons, we can wake up to all of the traps that detract from our happiness. In 1927, Walter Evans-Wentz translated an obscure Tibetan book called *The Tibetan Book of Living and Dying* that contains stories from a Tibetan teacher named Sogyal Rinpoche. The idea that life provides us with lessons and that we have choices is revealed in a section called "Autobiography in Five Chapters":

1.
I walk down the street.
There is a deep hole in the sidewalk,
I fall in.
I am lost...I am hopeless.
It isn't my fault.
It takes forever to find a way out.

2.
I walk down the same street.
There is a deep hole in the sidewalk,
I pretend I don't see it.
I fall in again.
I can't believe I'm in the same place.
But it isn't my fault.
It still takes a long time to get out.

3.
I walk down the same street.
There is a deep hole in the sidewalk,
I see it is there.
I still fall in...it is a habit.
My eyes are open.

I know where I am.
It is my fault.
I get out immediately.

4.
I walk down the same street.
There is a deep hole in the sidewalk,
I walk around it.

5.
I walk down another street.

- Sogyal Rinpoche
Autobiography in Five Chapters

Assertiveness Helps Strengthen Weak Boundaries

I've noticed that weak boundaries exist in families with parents who are either rigid and angry or extremely laid back. In either case, weak boundaries usually lead to confusion about the meaning of integrity. Twelve-step programs are often helpful for teaching codependents how to be assertive.

In the following examples, each of the codependents have reached a point in their lives where they are starting to take back their integrity:

Codependent/Situation	Positive Self-Talk	Possible Next Step
Jennifer: Jennifer, age 30, is married to a flaming alcoholic who has knocked over the Christmas tree and sworn at the kids for four years in a row. Finally, in the fifth year, she makes her husband leave and says, "I've had it!"	I am worthy of a wonderful, nurturing relationship. I can only change myself. I cannot control an alcoholic. My children also deserve a healthier life.	• Go to Al-Alon. • Try to stay away from any negative family and friends. • Find a personal support network or a group of family and friends who provide encouragement.
Marcia: Marcia, age 38, is living with a man who has spent all of her savings on drugs and gambling. She feels she's hit bottom and can't continue in her relationship.	I'm worthy of a good relationship. I'm in charge of my own happiness. I can only change myself.	• Leave the relationship. • Go to Al-Alon. • Work on her insecurities so that she becomes stronger (Note: Codependents have insecurities, or they would not be codependent).

Chapter 5

RULE #5

We Do Not Change Our Core Personality—We Just Learn to Work With It

"We have met the enemy and he is us."
- Pogo, Pogo Comic Strip

"After working with couples, individuals and groups for several years and after running several adolescent treatment centers, it became apparent to me that a person's core personality is not changeable. I also realized that extroverts had a lot of trouble understanding introverts and introverts had trouble communicating with extroverts. When I counseled couples, I realized that certain types of changes were impossible. For example, an introvert was never going to be an extrovert—and a very obsessive organized person was never going to be loose and bohemian."

Learning About Personality Types

Note:
A small amount of change in a person's personality is a possibility, but their core is not changeable.

As adults, we soon discover (through trial and error) that we really can't get anyone to change. Although a small amount of change is possible, each person has a core personality that is formed at a very young age. Core personality traits are formed between the age of 0-to-5 years and it is thought that a person's core may be, in part, genetically determined. Problems frequently occur when we ask someone to behave in a way that is not consistent with who they are at their core.

Personality Types

In my thirty years of counseling practice, I see conflicts in personality types most often in marriage counseling. Human beings are complex and there is a lot that lurks below the surface of who you initially interact with. Psychologist Carl Jung has provided us with theories of psychological types that were molded into personality preferences by Katherine Briggs and her daughter Isabel Myers. Together, they developed an extensive set of type indicators to help people identify personality preferences. Although most of the detail concerning the Myers-Briggs Type Indicators (MBTI) is beyond the scope of this book, I've added two derivative self-tests to this chapter to help readers learn about themselves. Although the personality profiles provide a theoretical understanding of who you are, don't consider each profile to be *set in stone*.

Ideas to Consider About Personality Types

Here are some important ideas to consider about personality tests in general:

Quote: "Man's main task in life is to give birth to himself, to become what he potentially is. The most important product of his effort is his own personality."

- Erich Fromm
  Psychoanalyst
  Social Theorist

Begin By "Typing" Yourself

William Shakespeare said, "To Thine Own Self Be True." Learning about your own personality preferences provides a tool for understanding who you are—and a concrete means to negotiate what you need from other people.

Myers-Briggs Values Differences

The Myers-Briggs profiles are neutral—none of the traits are *better* than others. The truth is that there are clear differences that exist among people and the Myers-Briggs system introduces us to *at least* 16 different types of personalities. In other words, there are at least 16 different types of *normal*.

Don't Use a Profile to Make Assumptions About Anyone

Although the Myers-Briggs profiles help you understand yourself and others, no two people with the same type are exactly alike. Within a given personality type, there are many variations. In addition, although personality traits are considered to be *inborn*, it is possible to *learn* opposite traits.

"X" Means "In Between Preference"

Most popularized versions of the Myers-Briggs personality profiles are a derivative of Kiersey Bates preferences that are first described in David Kiersey's and Marilyn Bates' book *Please Understand Me*. They use an "X" for people who do not have clear-cut preferences. An "X" is used in place of a letter for people who need an "I don't know" category. For example, if the test reveals you're an Introvert Intuitive Judger who's halfway between a "Thinker" and a "Feeler," you may be an INXJ instead of an INTJ or an INFJ. There are no actual tests that give an "X" result. Rather, this is a helpful way to describe an "in-between" preference.

Quote: "Life is a deck of cards, play with what you are dealt."

- Leonardo DiCaprio
Actor

Learn From Those Who Have Opposite Traits
Cultivating relationships with people who have opposite traits brings many benefits. Life settings and career paths often attract people with similar personality traits. People with the same type function as clones or lemmings. Lemmings are furry rodents that are known to follow each other over a cliff. It may be said that diversity positively prepares us for a dynamic, changing world. A broad collection of perspectives prevents us from stagnating.

It Takes Effort to Stretch Outside Your Box
When we make assumptions about another person's characteristics, traits and desires, we fail to recognize diversity. An understanding of types takes effort but it broadens our perception of the world. While it is much easier to stay inside our personal box and feel comfortable with what's familiar, you can't grow beyond the limits of a box. This creates blind spots that make us dull. Blind spots can also lead to missed opportunities.

How to Use This Chapter

Note:
It is very helpful to use the Myers-Briggs system and to learn your personality type letters.

The Myers-Briggs system offers us a tool in both our personal and professional life. However, in realizing that the degree to which readers will want to explore the subject will vary, I have organized this chapter as follows:

Basic Self-Test

This unofficial basic self-test will provide you with the Myers-Briggs personality code letters, of which there are 16 different combinations.

What I've Learned About Types

The stories I have to share don't cover all of the types. In fact, most of the conflicts seem to revolve around a couple of the types. The basic self-test is designed to get you acquainted with the building blocks of the personality types so that you understand the conflicts I've witnessed in marriage counseling.

Reference Sections Covering Type Preferences

These sections are not for everybody. They are meant to be directories for readers who want to explore the details of their own personality type and the personalities of those around them.

How to Proceed

If you're interested in exploring this subject, here's how to proceed:

Step #1. Take the Basic Self-Test

You will need to take the Basic Self-Test to determine your personality type letters. Together, these letters create

Quote: "You don't have to like each other, but you will learn to respect each other."

- Denzel Washington, Actor

a personality portrait. As you're taking the Basic Self-Test, write the letters down and use this *code* to look up the description of a profile in this chapter's Reference Sections.

Step #2. Notice How The Profiles Are Clustered
Carl Jung's extrovert and introvert characteristics are considered to be dominant temperament descriptions around which the other categories cluster. Realizing that all the Introvert profiles and all the Extrovert profiles are grouped together will help you navigate the *reference* sections and do look-ups. Here's a list of the four-letter codes and their longer profile names:

Introverts

Intuitives	• **INTJ** Introverted iNtuitive Thinking Judger
	• **INFJ** Introverted iNtuitive Feeler Judger
Thinkers	• **INTP** Introverted iNtuitive Thinking Perceiver
	• **ISTP** Introverted Sensor Thinking Perceiver
Sensors	• **ISTJ** Introverted Sensing Thinking Judger
	• **ISFJ** Introverted Sensing Feeler Judger
Feelers	• **ISFP** Introverted Sensing Feeler Perceiver
	• **INFP** Introverted iNtuitive Feeler Perceiver

FYI: "My best friend from childhood, Doug Loew, was about 13 years old when he said "Shilts, I've found the secret to life.""

I said, "What's that?"

To which he replied, "I've learned to enjoy my depressions!"

I said, "Oh really? How so?"

He said, "They teach me lessons."

I realize now Doug is an old soul.

Extroverts

Intuitives	•	**ENTP** Extroverted iNtuitive Thinking Perceiver
	•	**ENFP** Extroverted iNutuitive Feeling Perceiver
Thinkers	•	**ENTJ** Extroverted iNtuitive Thinking Judger
	•	**ESTJ** Extroverted Sensing Thinking Judger
Sensors	•	**ESTP** Extroverted Sensing Thinking Perceiver
	•	**ESFP** Extroverted Sensing Feeling Perceiver
Feelers	•	**ENFJ** Extroverted iNtuitive Feeling Judger
	•	**ESFJ** Extroverted Sensing Feeling Judger

Basic Self-Test

The Basic Self-Test contains four questions that will help you determine your personality type letters. Because there are 16 different combinations, these codes can seem a little overwhelming. The stories I have to share deal with the letters: Extrovert (E) and Introvert (I).

Quote: "Don't try to take on a new personality; it doesn't work."

- Richard M. Nixon

Directions:

After each question, respond with a yes if you feel that the question or statement describes your temperament.

If you would like to reuse this test, make a photocopy of the test before you mark the choices.

Question #1: Do you gain or drain energy when you're around other people?

This question is an important one because it describes *where* a person gains their personal energy.

Mark "yes" if the statement describes your temperament

Group interactions give you energy
You like to spend nearly all of your leisure time with other people
You feel deprived when you are cut off from other people
You enjoy being in the center of things
After socializing, you feel you need to spend time alone
You prefer to act immediately rather than weigh your choices when making decisions
You require quiet time when learning anything new

Quote: "Sometimes I feel an obligation to be accessible as a personality, but for me the driving force since the beginning has always been good work, taking risks, trying new things. If the door opens, go through it. Always go forwards."

- David Soul
Actor

Determining Your Personality Type Letter:
If you had:

Less than three yes responses, you are an Introvert (I).

Greater than three yes responses, you are an Extrovert (E)

Record the letter of the characteristic.

Question #2: When taking in information, do you prefer "just the facts" or do you enjoy exploring patterns and relationships between the facts?

This preference describes whether a person pays attention to data they gather from their five senses or they trust an inner voice that helps them develop hunches.

Mark "yes" if the statement describes your temperament

You usually notice new sights, sounds and smells
You're good at organization
You prefer to rely on your own experience rather than consider possible alternatives
You're detail oriented
You're not likely to make speculative guesses
You're uncomfortable when someone gives you "fuzzy" information
You're an inventor type who finds it easy to use your imagination

Determining Your Personality Type Letter:

If you had:

Less than three yes responses, you are an Intuitive (N).

Greater than three yes responses, you are a Sensor (S).

Record the letter of the characteristic.

Question #3: When you make a decision, do you focus on values such as fairness or harmony?

This preference describes how a person makes decisions. Thinkers rely on analysis and logic while Feelers rely on their feelings.

	Mark "yes" if the statement describes your temperament
As a student, you like courses that involve rote learning or critical thinking	
As a student, you enjoy large group interaction	
You wish you were better at picking up or sensing other people's reactions	
At work and at play, you find it easy to sort out tasks	
You're not bothered by conflict because you see it as a normal part of interacting with people	
You prefer facts and you rarely rely on personal feelings when making decisions	

Quote: "Fat, Drunk and Stupid is no way to go through life, son."

- Animal House

	Mark "yes" if the statement describes your temperament
You identify more with news anchor Jim Lehrer than you do with John Daly.	

Determining Your Personality Type Letter:
If you had:

   Less than three yes responses, you are a Feeler (F).

   Greater than three yes responses, you are a Thinker (T).

Record the letter of the characteristic.

Question #4: When you need to take action, are deadlines sacred or are they meant to be stretched?

This preference describes how a person likes to run his/her life. Are you driven by lists or are you spontaneous?

	Mark "yes" if the statement describes your temperament
Do you find it easy to complete tasks?	
As a student, do you do your homework right away?	
Are you most comfortable making moves with a plan?	
Do you like to stay ahead of deadlines?	

Quote: "There's very little advice in men's magazines, because men don't think there's a lot they don't know. Women do. Women want to learn. Men think, 'I know what I'm doing, just show me somebody naked.'"

- Jerry Seinfeld
  Entertainer
  (Introvert)

Mark "yes" if the statement describes your temperament

Do you like to create routines in your daily life?
Do you like to avoid time commitments?
Are you good at managing your time?

Determining Your Personality Type Letter:
If you had:

Less than three yes responses, you are a Perceiver (P).

Greater than three yes responses, you are a Judger (J).

Record the letter of the characteristic.

Extroverts Drive Introverts Nuts

Note:
People who have heard the expressions "introvert" and "extrovert" often think these words refer to a person's level of shyness. Although introverts may develop reputations as shy people, in reality it's because they need time alone to recharge their batteries. In contrast, extroverts need to charge their batteries around other people.

Jonathan Rauch, who writes for *The Atlantic Monthly*, recently wrote an article titled "Caring for Your Introvert – the habits and needs of a little-understood group." It's a humorous piece that explains introversion. He says, "Introverts are among the most misunderstood and aggrieved groups in America, possibly the world." Rauch explores the way introverts and extroverts process energy. As defined in the previous section, other people energize extroverts and they're drained when they're alone. In contrast, introverts wilt or fade when they're around other people and desperately need to turn off and recharge by themselves. Rauch calls himself an introvert and says that although he denied it for years, he finally *came out* to his friends and colleagues. His formula for recharging is two hours alone for every hour of socializing.

Introverts in Public Life

It's interesting to note who the introverts are in public life. David Remnick, a writer who works for *The New Yorker*, describes Al Gore as an introvert in a September 2004 article entitled "The Wilderness Campaign." Remnick quotes one of Gore's former aides, who says, "One thing about Gore personally is that he is an introvert. Politics was a horrible career choice for him. He should have been a college professor, a scientist or an engineer. He would have been happier. He finds dealing with other people draining. And so he has trouble keeping up his relations with people. The classic difference between an introvert and an extrovert is that if you send an introvert into a reception or an event with a hundred other people, he will emerge with less energy than he had going in; an extrovert

Quote: "If I'm not back in five minutes.. wait longer."

- *Ace Ventura,
Pet Detective*

will come out of that event energized, with more energy than he had going in. Gore needs a rest after an event. Clinton would leave invigorated because dealing with people comes naturally to him."

In "Caring for Your Introvert," Jonathan Rauch points out that the few introverts that rose to the top in politics were Calvin Coolidge, Richard Nixon and possibly Ronald Reagan, who was known for his privateness. Rauch says many actors are introverts and many introverts, when socializing, feel like actors. As a result, introverts are not "naturals" in politics.

" I need my alone time. From now on, I'll be available by e-mail."

Introverts and Extroverts as Couples

Note:
When couples do not understand the differences between an extrovert and an introvert, there can be a lot of friction.

Couples with opposite personality types can make adjustments in a marriage if they understand their partner's needs. I am an extrovert (ENFP) and my wife Bev is an introvert (ISTJ), and we have been married for thirty years. According to statistics, we should never have made it this far. I am definitely more comfortable around large groups of people—I have a wide variety of friends, feel at ease striking up conversations with strangers, have an occupation where I am continually interacting with others on a very personal level, I like spontaneity, and I also like to "wing it."

Bev, on the other hand, likes to socialize in smaller, more intimate settings. She has many acquaintances but only a few good friends (the oldest friendship is going on 50 years) and she would be more reticent about interacting with strangers in a public setting. She likes to organize her schedule, has chosen an occupation and hours that afford her brief interactions with the public, a minimum number of coworkers, and plenty of "down" time. I'm not afraid of conflict, like the exchange of different ideas, and tend to lead or surround myself with leader-types, while Bev is much more comfortable in the "power behind the scenes" position. Because of our different temperaments, we have learned to divide our couple "tasks" accordingly—an on-going learning process that hasn't always been smooth by any means.

Positive interactions are much more likely to occur when a couple learns about their partner's personality type. Jim and Jane are an example. When they came to see me, they explained that they had been together for three years and they had known each other for five years. When I asked

Quote: "If I were given the opportunity to present a gift to the next generation, it would be the ability for each individual to learn to laugh at himself."

- Charles M. Schulz
  Cartoonist

them both about their relationship, they explained that the differences in their personalities that had once felt exciting were now causing problems. Jim was an extrovert and Jane was an introvert. In the beginning, he liked how she listened to him and she liked the ease with which he met new friends. After four years, he was gone a lot and she spent a great deal of time alone. When they did spend time together, she felt drained and he felt rejected. She either fell asleep while they were talking or she would move into another room in their apartment.

When I describe the Myers-Briggs personality profile to couples that have opposite types, they understand the problem. Learning how to make adjustments takes time, but many couples succeed. Let's review extrovert and introvert characteristics:

Extroverts	Introverts
Prefers crowds and action	Avoids crowds
Feels energized after socializing	Feels drained after socializing
Has many casual acquaintances	Forms long-term relationships
Spontaneous talker	Weighs thoughts before speaking
More of a talker than a listener	More of a listener than a talker

Extroverts	Introverts
Anxious to make decisions	Needs time to process before making decisions
May feel rejected by an introverted partner	May feel "flooded" by an extroverted partner

Once extroverts and introverts learn what their partner's issues are, they can improve their relationship by developing the following strategies:

Extroverts	Introverts
Slow down and give your introverted partner time to process	Encourage your extroverted partner to have friends
Pick an occupation that is very suited to your personality type. This will take the pressure off your personal relationship.	Pick an occupation that is very suited to your personality type. This will take the pressure off your personal relationship.
Don't take offense or feel rejected if your introverted partner needs to be alone.	Look for tasks that provide alone time (e.g., sewing, cooking, reading, gardening, working on the car, etc.)

Quote: "Just once, I'd like for someone to call me 'sir' without adding 'you're making a scene.'"

- Homer Simpson

Note: The key to developing effective strategies of your own is to learn about your partner's personality profile and to understand his/her process.

Sometimes introverts and extroverts find it impossible to work out their differences. Robert Downey Jr. and Sarah Jessica Parker are an example. He's an extrovert, she's an introvert, and their relationship lasted seven years. They met when they were eighteen on the set of the movie *Firstborn* and lived in Parker's Upper West Side apartment before moving to Los Angeles. When interviewed for *GQ* Magazine, Sarah Jessica Parker says all their friends knew they had completely different personalities. His extroverted personality helped her find the courage to socialize. She remembers great Christmases and Thanksgivings when they cooked huge dinners for friends.

Meet Jerry

In "Caring for Your Introvert," Rauch says that extroverts are easy for introverts to understand, but that the reverse is seldom true. He says extroverts have "little or no grasp of introversion" and says they cannot imagine why someone would want to be alone. Because there are more extroverts than introverts, it's possible that most extroverts never notice introverts gasping for air. Rauch says, "introverts don't outwardly complain—they roll their eyes and silently curse the darkness."

Two of my business partners learned that they had very different personalities. Jerry, our accountant, was an extreme introvert and Ken, our marketing manager, was an extreme extrovert. Ken had manic tendencies that made Jerry cringe. Ken had no problem asserting himself in business and he assumed that others could be equally as assertive. In contrast, Jerry was much more contemplative and needed to spend a large amount of time alone. When Ken cornered Jerry in his office or in the hallway, I noticed Jerry's eye's glaze over and every bit of energy appeared to drain from his body. When Ken began to ask Jerry to make presentations at the bank and hold longer meetings, I knew I had to intervene. I said to Ken,

"Jerry won't be with us much longer."

Surprised, Ken said,

"I thought Jerry liked his job."

I said,

"The reason he's leaving is because he'll be dead in a week."

Quote: "There's nothing like
a family crisis, especially a
divorce, to force a person to re-
evaluate his life."

    - Michael Douglas
      Actor
      (Extrovert)

Ken, who never noticed any of Jerry's body language, said,

> "Is he sick?"

Knowing that Ken did not have a clue that he was draining the life out of Jerry's body and mind, I said,

> "You're killing him. It's called flooding. He doesn't have a chance."

Extroverts often misread introverts' body language as disinterest. In reality, introverts are drained by other people and charge their batteries when they're alone. Extroverts charge their batteries whenever they're around other people and they're drained when they're alone.

In the workplace, the differences between introverts and extroverts need to be resolved, or the introverts end up leaving. In *The Introvert Advantage: How to Thrive in an Extrovert World*, Dr. Marti Olsen Laney explains that introverts immerse themselves in projects and need uninterrupted blocks of time. In contrast, extroverts like to ask "quick questions" to satisfy their need for energizing breaks. Without realizing it, an extrovert manager could be satisfying this need through micromanagement and frequent meetings. Recognizing that there are probably one or more introverts in your midst, here are some policies that might help:

Quote: "Yes, I'm going to be the President of the United States. You know why? You think you can get chicks by being in the movies? You can really get chicks by being the President. "

- Ben Affleck
Actor
(Extrovert)

Situation	Possible Solution
Your introvert is constantly interrupted by staff members who pop their heads into his/her office with questions or comments.	**An office with a door** – Although this will make an introvert seem aloof, a door is often necessary for an introvert who needs blocks of time alone to complete his/her work and charge their energy.
The office introvert's desk is next to the office coffee machine, water cooler, copying machine or supply cabinet.	**Find a quiet corner for your introvert** - If your office does not have enclosed offices, protect your introvert by moving his/her desk far away from the "action." A screen or other form of wall divider is another option that creates a psychological partition. You might also consider offering an introvert the opportunity to telecommute.
Your extrovert managers micromanage with frequent meetings	**The "business huddle" solution** – Although business meetings are a fact of life, for the introvert long

Quote: "There are two types of people in this world, good and bad. The good sleep better, but the bad seem to enjoy the waking hours much more."

- Woody Allen
Entertainer

Situation	Possible Solution
(continued) Your extrovert managers micromanage with frequent meetings	meetings are equivalent to bloodletting. Firms with busy managers have invented the "business huddle" which is a stand-up meeting covering topics that can be discussed quickly rather than slowly. Huddles won't work for every meeting, but they're a helpful antidote for your office introverts who drain when they're around other people.

In our office, Jerry needed new boundaries drawn that would allow him to thrive. When I talked to Ken, we agreed that we did not want Jerry to leave the company. Here are the solutions we agreed upon:

- Ken would no longer "drop in" on Jerry. When he needed to see him, Ken would make an appointment.

- Ken would talk slower and limit his discussions to one or two topics.

- Meetings would be limited 15 to 30 minutes.

Details About Personality Types

Note:
This section provides details about personality types. Use it as a reference guide for understanding the personality characteristics of the people you know.

The purpose of the Myers-Briggs personality type profiles is to help people understand Carl Jung's theories about psychological types. All told, there are sixteen different personality types, and this section will help you understand the different profiles.

Introvert Reference Section

Recall that introverts draw their energy from the inside. They're drained by other people and they recharge when they're alone. This trait is at their core and they also possess other characteristics that may be organized around Carl Jung's key temperaments:

Introverts
Intuitives

Introverted iNtuitive Thinking Judger (INTJ)

INTJs are original, independent and often stubborn. They are driven by their own ideas and are often hard to read. In fields that interest them, they have power to organize a job and carry it out with or without help. When stressed, INTJs may find social interaction difficult.

Introverted iNtuitive Feeler Judger (INFJ)

INFJs are quietly forceful and conscientious. They understand psychic phenomena and can intuit good and evil. They have complex personalities and are hard to get to know. A strong empathy for others causes them to dislike conflict. They are respected for their firm principles about how to serve the common good.

Thinkers

Introverted iNtuitive Thinking Perceiver (INTP)

INTPs are sharp thinkers with critical analytical abilities. They are continuous scanners who exhibit precision in thought and language. They like solving problems with logic and analysis. INTPs retreat into books, have difficulty expressing emotions, and may be intellectual snobs. Their desire to understand the universe makes them excellent teachers.

Introverted Sensing Thinking Perceiver (ISTP)

ISTPs value privacy and sometimes keep important issues a secret. They're often loyal to colleagues but insubordinate to authority. Overly regulated situations can cause stress. ISTPs are frequent risk takers despite frequent injuries. They thrive on excitement and are subject to boredom.

Sensors

Introverted Sensing Thinking Judger (ISTJ)

Practical, logical and realistic, ISTJs are guardians of the community and family. They make up their minds about what should be accomplished and work toward it steadily regardless of distractions. Serious and quiet, they are reliable communicators who exhibit great strength. They earn success through thoroughness and may marry to rescue a spouse.

Introverted Sensing Feeling Judger (ISFJ)

Quiet and friendly, ISFJs are attracted to jobs that serve others. They are kindhearted, sensitive and thorough. They are the least hedonistic of all the types and enjoy assisting the downtrodden. They work to meet their obligations, adhere to established ways of doing things and prefer quiet, modest friends.

Feelers

Introverted iNtuitive Feeling Perceiver (INFP)

INFPs are calm on the outside and appear to be cool and detached. They do care deeply on the inside, responding to what is good and moral. Their natural ability to identify with others makes them full of loyalties. INFPs are little concerned with possessions or physical surroundings and are devoted to family.

Introverted Sensing Feeling Perceiver (ISFP)

ISFPs usually do not lead, but they are loyal followers who have a need to please everyone. They are artists by nature and are often drawn to music, painting and dancing. ISFPS are retiring, quiet, sensitive, kind and modest about their abilities. If their freedom is limited, they may become bored and passively defiant. They are often good athletes and are not interested in academics.

Quote: "It's very little trouble for me to accomodate my fans, unless I'm actually taking a pee at the time. "

> - Harrison Ford
>   Actor
>   (Extrovert)

Extrovert Reference Section

Recall that extroverts all draw their energy from other people. This trait is their core, and they also possess other characteristics that may be organized around Carl Jung's key temperaments:

Extroverts
Intuitives

Extroverted iNtuitive Thinking Perceiver (ENTP)

ENTPs provide stimulating company and are usually outspoken. Their interest in everything is contagious. They are talkative and good at motivating others, and consistently seek out new projects, activities and procedures. ENTPs are often resourceful in solving new problems and may neglect life's routine tasks. They are quick, ingenious and good at many things.

Extroverted iNtuitive Feeling Perceiver (ENFP)

ENFPs rely on their ability to improvise rather than prepare in advance, and they have difficulty working in a structured environment. They tend to procrastinate and move on to new projects without completing a project they have already started. ENFPs are scanners who have a strong sense of others' motivations and notice every detail. They avoid routine and need a conflict-free home.

Quote: "The simple act of paying attention can take you a long
way."

   - Keanu Reeves
     Actor
     (Extrovert)

Thinkers

Extroverted iNtuitive Thinking Judger (ENTJ)

ENTJs often have a strong urge for structure,
they're good planners, and they tend to be impatient with errors. They're tough-minded and
impervious to social customs. Frequently, they
are well informed and are good at anything that
requires reasoning and intelligence. They are
decisive leaders, they give tirelessly to a job, and
they enjoy responsibility.

Extroverted Sensing Thinking Judger (ESTJ)

ESTJs like to organize and run activities and are
very responsible. They like to see things done correctly and tend to be impatient as well as abrupt.
They are not interested in subjects they have no use
for and have a keen interest in tradition.

Sensors

Extroverted Sensing Thinking Perceiver (ESTP)

Good at spot problem-solving, ESTPs are outstanding entrepreneurs, diplomats and negotia-
tors but may be unaware of the consequences of
their actions. They are socially adept and have
great skill at detecting others' motives. They dislike long explanations and are most comfortable
with things that can be handled or taken apart.
They are witty, clever and fun but may be drawn
to swindling and counterfeiting if the desire for
excitement is not channeled into constructive
activities.

Quote: "Sometimes I lie awake at night, and I ask, 'Where have I gone wrong?' Then a voice says to me, 'This is going to take more than one night.'"

- Charlie Brown

Extroverted Sensing Feeling Perceiver (ESFP)

ESFPs are performers who radiate warmth, optimism and a joy of living. They like sports, love the limelight and have a need to socialize. They are outstanding at conversation and live on the edge of adventure. They are generous and impulsive and prefer active jobs with people. They have a low tolerance for anxiety and avoid anything that will bring them down.

Feelers

Extroverted iNtuitive Feeling Judger (ENFJ)

ENFJs are sociable, extremely tolerant of others and seldom critical. They are responsive to praise as well as criticism and can lead a group discussion with ease. As leaders, they may over-identify with the concerns of others and lose sight of their own interests. As skilled speakers, they are attracted to clergy, acting, writing and consulting.

Extroverted Sensing Feeling Judger (ESFJ)

ESFJs are restless when isolated from people. They need harmony and may be good at creating it. They are frequently attracted to service occupations and are often doing something nice for someone. Devoted to a traditional home, they are the most sociable of all types and enjoy dining. ESFJs will become very depressed if they are blamed for anything that is wrong in a relationship or an organization.

More Details About Each Type

Note:
People are often interested to know how many of each personality type are in the general population. For example, 75 percent of the population are extroverts. This section provides details about the number of subgroups. In addition, the personality types of famous people help us learn characteristics about each type.

To explore the Myers-Briggs personality types, this section includes details to help you learn more about each group.

How Many People Are Introverts?

The total number of introverts in the population is approximately 25 percent. Here is a chart that provides the percentage of each personality portrait:

Personality Type	Approximate Number in the Population
Introvert Intuitives	
INTJ	1%
INFJ	1%
Introvert Thinkers	
INTP	1%
ISTP	12%

Personality Type	Approximate Number in the Population
Introvert Sensors	
ISTJ	6%
ISFJ	6%
Introvert Feelers	
INFP	1%
ISFP	1%

Quote: "I made a commitment to completely cut out drinking and anything that might prevent me from getting my mind and body together. And the floodgates of goodness have opened upon me - spiritually and financially."

- Denzel Washington
  Actor
  (Introvert)

Personality Type	Approximate Number in the Population
Extrovert Intuitives	
ENTP	5%
ENFP	5%
Extrovert Thinkers	
ENTJ	5%
ESTJ	12%
Extrovert Sensors	
ESTP	13%
ESFP	13%
Extrovert Feelers	
ENFJ	5%
ESFJ	13%

Who's an Introvert?

Ever wonder who's an introvert? Many people consider celebrity profiles to be a useful study aid. The following list is a compilation of several lists available as public-domain data on the Internet (Note: The personality traits were compiled by people who are familiar with the MBTI system and not from actual test results):

Quote: "In my room as a kid... I'd play a fighter and get knocked to the floor and come back to win."

> - Dustin Hoffman
>   Actor
>   (Introvert)

Type	Celebrities
Introvert Intuitives	
INTJ	Alan Greenspan, Cuba Gooding, Jr., Ayn Rand, Mark Wahlberg and Donald Rumsfeld
INFJ	Oprah Winfrey, Lieutenant Worf (*Star Trek*), Calista Flockhart and Ralph Fiennes
Introvert Thinkers	
INTP	Albert Einstein, Dustin Hoffman, John Travolta, Friedrich Nietzsche and Lieutenant Commander Data (*Star Trek*)
ISTP	George Carlin, Ashley Judd, Meg Ryan, Goldie Hawn and Tommy Lee Jones
Introvert Sensors	
ISTJ	Anthony Hopkins, Julia Roberts, Sarah Jessica Parker and Denzel Washington
ISFJ	Jerry Seinfeld, William Shatner, Tyne Daly and Kiefer Sutherland
Introvert Feelers	
INFP	Kevin Costner, Deanna Troy (*Star Trek*) and Gillian Anderson
ISFP	Matt LeBlanc, Viggo Mortensen (Aragorn in *The Lord of the Rings*) and James Dean as Jim Stark (*Rebel Without a Cause*)

Who's An Extrovert?

The following chart includes celebrities and their Myers-Briggs personality portraits:

Type	Celebrities
Extrovert Intuitives	
ENTP	John Cleese, Dick Van Dyke, Jim Carrey and Cosmo Kramer (*Seinfeld*)
ENFP	Cher, James Woods, Keanu Reeves, Heather Locklear, Robin Williams and Captain Jonathan Archer (*Star Trek*)
Extrovert Thinkers	
ENTJ	Bill Gates and Harrison Ford
ESTJ	Bruce Willis, Brendan Fraser, Drew Carey and John Goodman.
Extrovert Sensors	
ESTP	Jack Nicholson, Peter Falk, Antonio Banderas and Madonna.
ESFP	Al Pacino, Joe Pesci, The Oracle (*The Matrix*), Ben Affleck, and Seamus Harper (Gene Roddenberry's *Andromeda*).
Extrovert Feelers	
ENFJ	Kelsey Grammer (*Fraser*), Michael Douglas, Sean Connery and Bette Midler
ESFJ	Eddie Murphy, Kate Mulgrew and Julia Louise Dreyfus.

How Much Do Opposites Attract?

Note:
Strangely enough, research suggests that opposites do not marry.

An American Psychological Association (APA) study says that similar personality types are much more likely to stay married and be happier with their selection. In 1996, the APA presented the results of a research study that explored personality types and marital satisfaction. Psychologist Nancy S. Marioles, Ph.D. of St. Mary's University and five other researchers monitored 426 married and premarried couples for seven years. They examined how many times each person was married, the length of the marriage, the changes of marital status and the sources of marital satisfaction. The researchers found:

- Opposites usually do not marry. Exceptions included:

   - ESTJ men married to INFP women
   - ESTP men married to INFJ women

- ESTJ and ESTP men married the most often

- INFP, INFJ and INTP men most often married women with the same personality type

- ENFJ and INFJ women most often married men with the same type

- ESFJ females (feeling types) were married the longest

- INTP females (thinking types) were married the fewest number of years

- Perceiving types divorced more than judging types

- Extroverts were more satisfied than introverts regardless of how many times they were married

- The largest numbers of women dissatisfied with marriage included:

   - Women married to INTP men (33%)
   - Women married to INFS men (31%)
   - Women married to ISFP men (22%)

Quote: "He who laughs most, learns best."

- John Cleese
  Entertainer
  (Extrovert)

- The largest number of men dissatisfied with marriage included:

  - Men married to ENFJ women (13%)
  - Men married to ENFP women (12%)

Introvert Flash Cards to Use When an Extrovert Is Flooding You

Note:
Extroverts often do not understand introverts.

Katherine, who is one of my extroverted patients, created a set of flash cards that can be presented to extroverts when they're flooding an introvert.

If you'd like to make a set of Katherine's cards for your extrovert, photocopy this page on a piece of heavy cardstock paper and cut them out.

Dear Extrovert,

Please be quiet.

Please be quiet.

Please be quiet.
Signed, Introvert

Extrovert...

Breath in…Breath out…
Breath in…Breath out…

Repeat

Extrovert Alert!

This would be an excellent time for a moment of silence.

Make that several moments of silence...

Extroverts are the most wonderful people...

Especially when they are reading, sleeping, meditating, traveling in distant lands, gardening in their own yards, chewing taffy and studying alone...

Notes

Chapter 6

RULE #6

The First Contracts in Marriage Usually Need to Be Renegotiated

The keys to working things out in a relationship:

- *Face your own truths about yourself*
- *Face truths about the other person*
- *Manage the friction*

"Over the years, I noticed that the couples who connected very early in their lives often had immature relationships years later. These couples taught me a great deal about initial needs contracts that exist when we form relationships with our partners.

Many times, people get together because of unmet needs in their family of origin. When there's a shift in life circumstances, the change often causes a need for the marriage contract to change and that's difficult to do. I discovered that the first contract in a marriage rarely changes—unless there's a lot of stress and strain."

Why Couples Get Together...

Note:
Very early in my practice, I noticed that couples' marriage contracts were linked to their needs in their family of origin. It was clear that the first contract had to do with what a person did not receive or what they needed to complete. For example, a woman who never got along with her rigid father could marry a rigid man to try and get him to be less rigid.

It's said that we marry a parent of the opposite gender. I don't think it has anything to do with gender. It has more to do with marrying the opposite disposition of the parent with whom you identify the most. I call this marrying an *opposite identified parent*. In my case, my mother and I are both extroverts and we both married introverts.

Director/screenwriter Cameron Crowe's *Jerry Maguire* contains a deceptively romantic line that describes why most couples get together:

"You complete me..."

Early in the movie, Jerry (Tom Cruise) and his costar Dorothy (Renee Zellweger) meet a deaf couple in an elevator who are signing. Zellweger understands sign language and when Jerry asks her what they said, she says they signed, "You complete me." Jerry later uses this line in his own life when he needs to communicate to Zellweger why he loves her.

Whether or not a couple is aware of the reason they get together, the reason may be considered a *contract*. Some psychologists believe that there are really three entities in a marriage—the two individuals and their *relationship*. As time goes by, the individuals may change outside the relationship, but their relationship rarely changes.

Changing an Original Marriage Contract

Writer Shel Silverstein delves into the search for completeness in two of his books: *The Missing Piece* and *The Missing Piece Meets the Big O*. Silverstein wrote children's books, but his stories contain deep issues that adults can appreciate. These two small books have been endlessly discussed.

The Missing Piece
In *The Missing Piece*, Silverstein's story deals with a circle that has a wedge missing from its body. The

Quote: "I don't think it's necessarily healthy to go into relationships as a needy person. Better to go in with a full deck.

- Anjelica Huston
  Actress

circle searches to find its missing piece but after several mismatches, it finds that it was happier without the piece filled in.

The story of *The Missing Piece* has many correspondences. Here are a few *constants* that I've observed in my thirty years of counseling couples about their marriages:

- Couples sometimes believe that they're made for each other but soon discover that they really don't *fit*. Thomas Hardy, a nineteenth-century English poet and novelist, wrote, "The fundamental error of a matrimonial union is to base a permanent contract on a temporary feeling."

- If a couple marries and if one or both of the individuals grows, the growth causes a mismatch. In the search for completeness, two people find that they fit together and form a contract. When someone grows, the original contract no longer works (the circle and piece no longer fit).

- If you don't grow, you may keep remarrying the same person (the same mismatch). In fact, they may even look the same. A famous example is John Derek. He married Ursula Andress, Linda Evans and Bo Derek—women who looked very much alike.

The Missing Piece Meets The Big O

The Missing Piece Meets the Big O is about a piece that longs to find a circle to *roll with*. When it finds that they can no longer roll together, the Big O tells the piece to roll on its own. At first, the piece finds this hard but as its edges wear down, rolling becomes easier and easier. Soon, they're both round and they can roll together.

This time, the Big O and the piece work at changing their original contract. They reach a point where they can no longer roll together but they're willing to help each other, perhaps with the help of some counseling. The piece will help the Big O fill in an indentation and the Big O will help the piece polish corners.

After 30 Years of Marriage Counseling...

Here's what I've learned from counseling couples about their marriages:

- Changing the original contract is *very hard*.

- Filling in an indentation and polishing corners represents healing. Couples *can help each other heal.*

- When couples succeed, heal and change their contract, it's almost as though the contract and people involved are all new.

Meet Mike and Joan

Note:
It always amazed me that couples can be very mature outside of their marriage relationship, but if they married at a very young age, their relationship does not mature.

Mike and Joan are an example of a couple that tried to change their original contract but could not succeed. When they came to see me, they had been in a tumultuous marriage for 20 years. There was a theme in their relationship that was a constant throughout the twenty years—he ran away and she chased him to try to control what she called his "immature behavior." They had both achieved success in their careers but their personal life was always in trouble. He had his Ph.D. and worked as a business consultant, and she was a successful realtor.

Mike and Joan first met when he was 15 and she was 14. He was from a wealthy family but was very well rounded and not a status seeker. His friends came from all social circles, including his best friend who lived in a trailer. Joan came from a poor background and her objective in life was to improve her social status and associate with the community's upper class. Through their college years, he attended a private school and she attended a state college.

They had tried counseling many times, and had also gone to several encounter groups. Mike came to the first meeting alone at the insistence of his wife and gave me an overview of his rocky relationship. I asked Mike why he stayed in a relationship that was tumultuous.

"I never thought I was very good-looking and she was a beautiful girl who cared about me. I thought of her as a stabilizing force in my life.

Although I did not ask Mike about Joan's intentions, he commented on what he felt were her reasons for staying in the relationship.

> "I think she saw me as exciting, and I was able to help her move out of her poor social background."

When Mike made an appointment to see me, he had just ended an affair with one of his colleagues. It was not his first transgression and he commented on Joan's reaction to his affairs.

> "Joan always stalks the women I'm involved with. She knows every detail about their lives. I've been cheating on Joan since junior high school. She always does this."

Later, at a meeting with both partners present, I asked Joan why she stayed in the relationship if Mike constantly cheated on her.

> "I love him. Besides, don't all men cheat?"

I asked her if she had ever had a relationship with a man she could trust.

> "Not really. I don't know any men who don't cheat. My father drank a lot and he ran around on my mother. My girlfriends all have boyfriends and husbands who cheat."

Mike followed with details about his home life:

"I was an only child and my mother did not work outside the home. I was her 'project.' I see women as manipulative and controlling. I guess I was used to behavior like Joan's. However, the older I get, I realize I need a less controlling and more of a trusting, adult-type relationship. I don't need a mother anymore."

I asked Mike what it was exactly that makes him run away from Joan.

"Joan spends her time getting her nails done, getting tanned and drinking margueritas with all the 'important people.' I don't like country clubs, gossip or the 'upper class.' Joan thrives on it. I hate cocktail parties. I'd much rather spend my spare time building houses with my buddies."

Next, I asked Mike what it was that kept them together.

"We have two great kids and Joan is a really wonderful mother. I like being in a family. It's the one thing we do well together. I like parenting and I think we're both good at it."

At that point, Joan spoke up and said,

"Most of what Mike said is true—though I would be much less controlling if he stopped cheating."

I asked both of them about the differences in their values. Joan answered by saying:

"I think he needs to grow up."

When I asked her to explain, she said,

"He needs to act like a mature executive—like someone with status. He needs to quit fooling around. I've been trying to get him to grow up forever."

Next, I asked her if that meant that he should change to fit her values and she said:

"Yes, he needs to grow up."

Mike and Joan did not need to have many meetings in my office before I realized that they had been bouncing back and forth in a disengaged existence for 20 years. The only good connection they had was their children.

I told Mike and Joan that they needed to do some extensive self-evaluation and think about whether they were each willing to change—to become what the other person needed. I asked them both to look at their original contract and to consider whether it was still working. When they returned two weeks later, they told me they had made a decision to separate and they asked me to help them through their transition with their children. Two years later, I ran into Joan. She told me she was happily married to a doctor and that Mike had married a colleague. She said their children were doing fine.

Lyrics:

Every generation

Blames the one
before

And all of their frustrations

Come beating on your door

I know that I'm a prisoner

To all my Father held
so dear

I know that I'm a hostage

To all his hopes and fears

I just wish I could have told him
in the living years

Crumpled bits of paper

Filled with imperfect thought

Stilted conversations

I'm afraid that's all
we've got

> - Mike and the
> Mechanics
> *The Living Years*

In a relationship, the details of a marriage contract are always understood—whether consciously or subconsciously. It's possible that the individuals may never have communicated their thoughts and ideas about a contract—or why they got together. Without open communication, much of the detail exists on a subconscious level. When couples learn how to communicate in counseling sessions, the details of a marriage contract can be brought to the surface.

As a therapist, I explain to my clients that it is not my job to save a marriage or to advise them to dissolve their relationship. I help individuals clarify what they each want and I help them understand their first contract—to see if it is still working or if it can be successfully changed. It's important to understand that change in a marriage contract is possible only if the individuals are willing to change.

Quote: "Whenever you're in conflict with someone, there is one factor that can make the difference between damaging your relationship and deepening it. That factor is attitude."

- William James
   American Philosopher

"Honey, as long as you have some free time, could you pick up some golf balls, get the car washed and pick up a birthday present for my sister?"

Meet Jim and Carrie

Note:
Transference is very powerful and it can skew your thinking in extreme ways. Until you understand a person's internal frame of reference, you really can't understand their behavior.

As partners in a marriage grow, friction is often the result. Ironically, it's life's difficulties that make us grow. The Chinese have an appropriate expression:

> "The gem cannot be polished without friction, nor man perfected without trials."

Typically, when we transfer our family issues and project them onto a marriage partner, the issues that are triggered cause friction. In Shel Silverstein's book, *The Missing Piece Meets the Big O*—filling in an indentation and polishing corners represents healing. Couples can help each other heal. Jim and Carrie are an example. I first met Jim in individual counseling. When he came to see me, he said,

> "My wife said I need to take care of my temper and abusive behavior or she would leave."

Surviving Friction in a Marriage

Jim and Carrie had known each other since high school and they had been together for twenty-five years. Jim had seen many therapists and knew exactly how to summarize his childhood.

> "I was raised in a guerrilla war zone. I was the middle child in a family of seven boys. Dad was very abusive. I witnessed more abuse than I received. We were Catholics, and I call myself a 'recovering Catholic.' My mother was always shaming us for poor grades, messy bedrooms and not saying prayers. Her screaming was a cover-up.

Quote: "In her book *Adult Children of an Alcoholic*, Janet Geringer Woititz describes the dysfunctional characteristics of those who grow up in an alcoholic home:

- Adult children of alcoholics guess at what normal behavior is.
- Adult children of alcoholics have difficulty following a project through from beginning to end.
- Adult children of alcoholics lie when it would be just as easy to tell the truth.
- Adult children of alcoholics judge themselves without mercy.
- Adult children of alcoholics have difficulty having fun.
- Adult children of alcoholics take themselves very seriously.
- Adult children of alcoholics have difficulty with intimate relationships.

It distracted us from Dad's drinking. As a kid, I was very aware and nervous most of the time. I felt my job was to make sure that Dad would not blow up. I watched him beat my brothers and then my brothers beat me up. I learned not to trust myself. I think I'm pretty bright. My other therapists have told me I have good abstract reasoning."

I asked Jim about his goal for our therapy sessions.

"I want to be able to trust and be honest in my relationships. I don't want you to let me get away with anything. I have a habit of telling others what they want to hear. I need this counseling to work—this is my last chance."

I told Jim that the only way therapy can work is with trust. I told him I thought it looked as though he was beginning to trust because of all the details he provided. I asked him to tell me about his wife Carrie.

"Carrie is very demanding and angry. Her personality reminds me of my mother and father's personality rolled into one. She wants me to agree with her on every issue and she's very uncompromising. When we argue, I either blow up and get abusive or I give in and feel resentful. I can never win. If I blow up and get abusive, I feel extremely guilty and if I give in, I feel wimpy."

I told Jim the image of Carrie he described made it sound as though she was a muscle-bound hulk with a

Quote: "We humans have a wonderful mechanism that allows us to only feel as much pain as we can handle without becoming overwhelmed. Pain that is too great is put into our 'denial bag' and held until we are strong enough to experience and learn from it."

- Rebuilding When Your Relationship Ends
Dr. Bruce Fisher

booming voice. He laughed and said he was David and she was Goliath. I asked him about her early home life.

"Carrie came from a very abusive home. Her parents were emotionally neglectful and her mother was a troublemaker whom no one could contradict. Carrie was a rebel who fought for herself and her siblings."

When I met Carrie in person, I was stunned. She's a petite, quiet woman who is physically disabled with severe back problems. She spends a great deal of time lying down and in our sessions, she spent a great deal of time crying. Jim had talked about her hard side but never mentioned her soft side. They had each projected their family experiences on their partner:

Carrie	Jim
Carrie did not trust adults and projected this on Jim. She viewed him as someone who tried to control her. She had fought him as she had fought her mother.	He viewed Carrie as an amalgamation of his abusive mother and father. In Jim's eyes, Carrie *became* his abusive father when she would not listen.
Contract: She would love him enough to make up for his childhood abuse. They would heal each other and be OK.	**Contract:** He would take care of her because she had low self-esteem.

Lyrics:

(Son)

How can I try to explain, when I do he turns away again.

It's always been the same, same old story.

From the moment I could talk I was ordered to listen.

Now there's a way and I know that I have to go away.

I know I have to go.

- Cat Stevens
  Father and Son

Jim and Carrie's Second Contract

Jim and Carrie's contract became crazy when they both transferred their childhood issues onto the other person. They worked on modifying their contract through conflict resolution exercises in counseling sessions and at home. The work they did in counseling allowed them to heal their wounds, and to grow and form a new contract that included a new agreement. Although their first marriage contract was unspoken, their second contract contained elements that Jim and Carrie spoke about many times. Jim and Carrie would:

- Support each other's growth

- Respect each other

- Be responsible for their own growth (replacing their codependent tendency to make the other person "OK")

Detective Work: Why Did You and Your Partner Get Together?

Note:

Although the reason couples get together is often couplex, if they think very hard, they can usually figure it out. The quality of their parents' marriages often provides clues. I've also observed that what attracts people to each other at the beginning is what eventually creates the discord between them, i.e, why you marry a person may also be why you divorce them.

The contract that you formed with a partner is really a reflection of your needs and your partner's needs. As people grow, their needs change and they often outgrow their original contract. If you do some detective work to get in touch with why you and your partner got together, you'll learn:

- details about your past and present needs as well as your partner's needs

- how people select partners based on unfulfilled needs from his/her childhood

- that life's challenges cause growth and that growth causes change

Standard Contracts: Do Any of These Sound Familiar?

While you're thinking about the reasons you and your partner got together, you may be interested in a list of what I call "standard contracts." I call them standard because I've seen these patterns in couples over and over. The list is comprised of genderless "needs" that we'll attribute to "Person A" and "Person B:"

Person A	Person B
A needs excitement but likes a calming influence.	B needs stability but likes excitement.
If A loves B enough, he/she will make up for B's childhood.	A is a replacement for B's family of origin.
If A loves B enough, he/she will stop drinking.	If A stops nagging, then B will stop drinking.

Quote: "These things that I write about, not only have I experienced them but they are unavoidable. If you're any kind of human, you are going to have relationships."

- Nick Hornby
  Musician

Person A	Person B
A needs someone to take care of him/her.	B feels important when he/she is taking care of A.
A needs social status.	B has a partner who puts up with his/her flaws in return for social status (e.g., B cheats on A).
A is an introvert who needs a front person.	B is an extrovert who needs a good listener.
A needs focusing.	B needs to help someone focus.
A is scattered and needs help getting organized.	B needs a project in order to feel good about himself/herself.
We (A and B) need to recover together.	We (A and B) need to recover together.
A needs to keep B away from drugs and alcohol.	B needs someone who will take care of him/her.
If A takes care of B, B will eventually take care of A.	B never changes or grows up.
A needs to make B the best person he/she can be.	B needs to make A the best person he/she can be. *Note:* This couple is codependent. The key is the word "make." The word "support" would be healthier.

What to Do When a Shift Occurs...

Note:

Change is one of the most fundamental teachings of Buddhism. Buddhists consider impermanence to be a law that is basic to the world we live in. In relationships as in life, the only constant is change.

My own contract (with myself) is the pursuit of reality at any cost. Along with this, I try to be honest and forthright at all times.

It is easier to face change in life if we:

- *understand our own contract before we get involved with another person*

- *form a contract that is flexible and in the process, help our spouse become all that they can be by loving them in a loving and caring way.*

As you might have guessed, contracts are disrupted when changes occur in a marriage. Changes may occur due to personal growth or external circumstances. When shifts occur, couples usually need to:

Negotiate a New Contract

Changes in a marriage cause friction requiring couples to agree to mutually agreeable changes in their original contract. Over the course of a lifetime, marriage contracts often need to be renegotiated several times. My wife Bev and I have renegotiated our contract several times. If the relationship is important to both partners, they will want to make the necessary adjustments.

Split and Go Separate Ways

According to Luke Metcalfe, Manager/Developer of Rapid Intelligence, a Web technology company in Sydney, Australia, the divorce rate in the United States is the highest in the world. If more newlyweds understood that their marriage contact would need to be renegotiated, they would be better prepared for changes as they occur. Instead, couples often think that their problems are unique. After working as a mental health counselor for over 30 years, I know there are patterns, and many couples experience similar forms of stress. When I explain this to people who are experiencing marital stress, it's often comforting for them to learn that they are not alone. Let's look at examples of shifts that can cause friction in a relationship:

Person A	Person B	Change or Shift
A needs excitement but likes a calming influence.	B needs stability but likes excitement.	A mellows out and B gets bored, or A keeps going and B gets tired of the excitement.
If A loves B enough, he/she will make up for B's childhood.	A is a replacement for B's family of origin.	B grieves and no longer needs a replacement.
If A loves B enough, he/she will stop drinking.	If A stops nagging, then B will stop drinking.	B gets sober and A no longer has an alcoholic to take care of.
A needs social status.	B has a partner who puts up with his/her flaws in return for social status (e.g., B cheats on A).	B loses his high-salaried job.
A is an introvert who needs a front person.	B is an extrovert who needs a good listener.	A becomes more social and no longer needs a front person, or B refuses to acknowledge that introverts have different needs.
A is scattered and needs focusing or help getting organized.	B needs to help someone focus.	A and B have children and B no longer has time to help A.
We (A and B) need to recover together.	We (A and B) need to recover together.	The pace of recovery is different for A and B.
A needs to keep B away from drugs and alcohol.	B needs someone who will take care of him/her.	B grows up and no longer needs a mother.

Marriage Is a Two-Person Sport

Note:

After many years of marriage counseling, I posed the question:

"Why should anyone get married?"

The answer I came up with is to be part of a team that faces the world and life together.

I think the very best partner is someone who will "cover your back."

When I counsel couples about marriage, I explain that the only reason to be married is to be part of a team that faces life together. Facing the world together is a lot like partnering in a team sport. Think about how the players in each of the following sports must work with his/her partner:

- doubles tennis

- baseball (the catcher and the pitcher)

- volleyball

- ping pong

- racquetball

The two-person teamwork required in each of these examples requires that the individuals work together and not independently.

In previous chapters, we have repeatedly referred to the unfinished family of origin business that is frequently experienced in an intimate relationship. Although there is friction in all relationships, the person you choose as a life partner should be someone whom:

- you trust

- is an ideal team member who will "watch your back"

- has complementary skills in the long term

- has skills that will strengthen the skills you already have

- has good communication skills

Learning How to Be a Good Team Member

One of my sons plays two-person team sports, and the concepts that hold partners together on an athletic team can also hold married people together. It is commonly known that the principles of teamwork spread from the world of sports to business, but the ideas are also helpful in personal relationships.

John Maxwell, a bestselling author who writes about teamwork in sports, draws attention to couples working together in his book *The 17 Indisputable Laws of Teamwork Workbook*. In his first chapter, he includes a story about Brandon and Lily Tartikoffs' and their personal challenges.

When they met, Lily was a ballet dancer with the New York City Ballet Company and Brandon had just become the youngest-ever president of NBC Entertainment. They were married two years later—the same year that Brandon was diagnosed with Hodgkins Lymphoma for the second time in his life. While working to turn around NBC's low prime-time reputation with several series that would become the most successful shows in television, Brandon was also receiving treatment for his cancer. For a year, Brandon would take treatments on Fridays and Lily would take care of him through the weekends while he dealt with the side effects of his therapy. The support Brandon had in his marriage to Lily helped him achieve success at NBC. Brandon's career, now called the "Tartikoff era" brought us *The Cosby Show, Cheers, Hill Street Blues, St. Elsewhere, Miami Vice, The Golden Girls* and *the A-Team*.

The day-to-day behavior that's required for becoming a good team member is similar to what is required of

Lyrics:

Maybe I'm
just too demanding (maybe,
maybe, I'm like my father)

Maybe I'm just like my father
too bold (ya know he's too bold)

Maybe you're just like my
mother (maybe you're just like
my mother)

She's never satisfied (she's never,
never
satisfied)

Why do we scream at each other
(why do we scream why)

This is what it sounds like

When doves cry

When doves cry (doves cry,
doves cry)

- Prince
  When Doves Cry
  Purple Rain Album

an artist who strives to be creative. He/she needs to put their whole self into the endeavor. Although every relationship is unique, here are some tips I've learned from sports coaches:

Positivity Pays Off

In his book *Positive Coaching*, Jim Thompson says, "The things that get rewarded get done." This principle holds true in relationships as much as it does on a sports team. Thompson explains that when people are yelled at or criticized, their emotional energy is used up while they're feeling angry or feeling sorry for themselves. In a marriage or intimate partnership, the behavior adjustments that are often needed will be effortless if there's positive emotional support.

"Yeah, we finally got married but we need to renegotiate our contract."

You Are the Architects of Your Own Contract

Note:

When I counsel families, I tell them that the parents are the architects of their own marriage and that they need to take responsibility for building the home. As we have come to understand, this is a very powerful responsibility because the work that they do will be the foundation for future generations.

To guide their decision making, the Iroquois nation would consider the next seven unborn generations. They used this decision making principle 800 years before our forefathers created our constitution.

The details in a marriage contract are unique to the partners who create the contract. In marriage counseling sessions, I'm the consultant. The partners are the architects. They build their house and figure out how it works. I can only offer broad strokes, such as:

- Learn what your partner needs and try to anticipate his/her needs as you face life together

- Tell your partner what you need

- Define each team member's role (decide what you're both good at and what you're not good at).

- If there's a role that's missing (one that neither of you are good at), try to tackle this together or find help

- Be flexible on life's minor issues

- Be open, honest and vulnerable to support the growth of your team

Chapter 7

RULE #7

Life's Answers Are Found in the Struggle Between People

Effective communication is essential to understanding

"Invariably, we're always dealing with other people. Even when we're trying to work something out in our minds and no one is in the room, we almost always pull someone into our imagination."

Learning to Communicate

Note:

As youths, we are very much like immigrants from a foreign culture in that we have only minimal communication skills. Both our physical and emotional well-being are dependent on our ability to learn customs and culture.

Studies in England have shown that infants with no early physical contact can die. It's called "failure to thrive."

In many ways, contact and communication with other human beings is critical. Those who don't learn to communicate may not physically die—but their spirit may.

Remember the Newlywed Game? Four recently married couples answered questions designed to reveal how much they knew about each other. The game show seemed to capitalize on contestants' responses that were mostly goofs or answers that the audience found hilariously funny—revealing that they really did not understand their spouse. Unfortunately, the show also became famous for arguments that couples had over their incorrect answers that led to some divorces. The show's legendary 34-year run started in July, 1966, with several other versions produced through 1997.

Intimate Relationships Provide a Context for Healing

In Chapter 3, we discussed the tendency to transfer family issues to a marriage partner. Close intimate relationships provide a context for healing the unresolved issues of our childhoods—but there is nearly always friction involved.

Surviving friction in a marriage involves learning good communication skills. The same tools that are useful in a marriage may also be used in any one-on-one relationship. By developing new communication patterns, two parties involved in a conflict can try to break out of repetitive patterns that often crop up during times of stress.

Effective vs. Ineffective Communication

Quality communication is based on several basic assumptions, including:

Power and Control
Power and control issues are both impediments to quality communication.

Quote: "You know, it's at times like this when I'm stuck in a Vogon airlock with a man from Betelgeuse, and about to die of asphyxiation in deep space, that I really wish I'd listened to what my mother told me when I was young."

"Why, what did she say?"

"I don't know, I didn't listen."

- Douglas Adams
  The Hitchhiker's Guide
  to the Galaxy

Winning or Being Right

Communication suffers if one or both parties feel the need to win or be "right."

Agree to Disagree

Certain issues may never be resolved. At such times, it's perfectly OK to "agree to disagree."

Competition to Speak or Too Many Nonverbal Gestures

When one or more of the parties insists on speaking (or refuses to speak), communication breaks down. Quality communication requires that both parties become good speakers and good listeners.

Pitfalls to Good Communication

Repetitive conflicts sometimes go on for years causing a tremendous amount of hurt and anger. Learning to spot the road blocks of good communication can often lead to the development of more effective patterns.

Judgment

Casting blame or shame on the other party can cause great harm. Communication requires respect and consideration that is impossible to achieve when there is criticism. Watch for messages that contain the words "but, if, should or ought."

Disinterest

Disinterest in the form of verbal or nonverbal communication leads to conflict and despair and is almost impossible to resolve. Nonverbal body language that conveys disinterest includes lack of eye contact, restless shifting, rolling the eyes or walking away.

Quote: "Knowledge speaks, but wisdom listens."

- Jimi Hendrix

Ax grinding

Ax grinding occurs when one or more of the parties complain about the other person over and over.

Stored up emotions

Stored-up emotions can lead to resentment and open combat when one or more of the partners habitually mask their feelings.

Jumping to conclusions

Drawing a conclusion without adequate facts is a negative pattern that impedes problem solving in a relationship. This pitfall includes mind reading, which is an expectation that you know what your partner is thinking or feeling—or, you expect him/her to know what you are thinking or feeling.

Little or no positive reinforcement

Failure to give and receive appreciation is a sign that one or more of the parties has forgotten positive points about their partner.

Wandering off topic

Wandering off topic may be unintentional or deliberate and may lead to a *parallel fight*. This expression refers to a separate fight that develops over a second, emotionally charged topic. Parallel fights block resolutions because the parties jump to a second topic before they resolve the subject of their first fight.

Ultimatums

An ultimatum is a threat or a demand that is used in an attempt to get your way. Such an attempt to control a partner usually causes counterattack or withdrawal.

Quote: "Learn the art of patience. Apply discipline to your thoughts when they become anxious over the outcome of a goal. Impatience breeds anxiety, fear, discouragement and failure. Patience creates confidence, decisiveness and a rational outlook, which eventually leads to success."

- Brian Adams
How to Succeed

Insults

Insults, mocking remarks and sarcasm are all very destructive to a relationship. Hostile language can lead to physical intimidation and a complete breakdown in a relationship.

Impatience

Impatience with your partner demonstrates an inability to show support and may show up in the form of:

- Whining
- "Yeah buts"
- Interrupting
- Silent treatment

"We're working on our non-verbal communication skills."

Tools for Better Communication

Note:

In my thirty years as a mental health counselor, it has always amazed me how little training there is in communication skills. I'm also amazed at how well people learn new commnication skills when it is in their best interest to do so.

All of the communication tools described in this chapter revolve around the following goals:

1. Identifying and labeling feelings (Scaling Tool)

2. Expressing your feelings #1 (I Message Tool)

3. Expressing your feelings #2 (Assertive Message Tool)

4. Accepting another's feelings and avoiding the trap of invalidation (Validation Tool)

5. Paying attention (Active Listening Tool)

6. Preventing a conflict (Time-Out Tool)

For people who come from dysfunctional families (80 to 90 percent of us) these goals will require practice. To help with this, I've provided step-by-step sections for all of the different tools.

In *EQ for Everybody*, author Steve Hein explains that without an awareness of our feelings and what causes them, it is impossible to lead a happy life. People with a low emotional intelligence (EQ) lack high EQ role models, or the proper instruction. Most people with a low EQ do not lack an ability. Emotional intelligence can be learned. Identifying a feeling and labeling it as specifically as possible is an important first step.

Tool #1: Scaling (Identifying Your Feelings)

Note:
Women are usually very good at identifying their feelings. I've discovered that most women can identify five feelings before a man can identfy one.

This is an introduction to feeling words. Researchers tell us that there are four basic feelings:

- Mad
- Glad
- Sad
- Afraid

Our feelings about each of these states were programmed in our childhood. If any of these feelings were not accepted in your childhood, chances are you will have a hard time accepting the feeling as an adult—and may also have a difficult time recognizing it. As a first step, you'll learn to attach a number and a word to these four basic emotions.

Realize that if you decide to express your feelings to another person, he/she may reject the feelings you've expressed. Each person must assume responsibility for his/her own feelings. Honesty is an appropriate step on the road to quality communication.

Steps to Scale

When you first learn to scale, you may need to find a quiet place to listen to your emotions. With practice, you will be able to get in touch with your feelings instantly.

Scaling/Step #1
Identify a situation that's uncomfortable

The body has a way of expressing pent-up emotions as physical symptoms. If we feel stress in response to some situation in our lives, chances are we are not in touch with a related emotion.

Quote: "Some people listen to themselves rather then listen to what others say. These people don't come along very often, but when they do, they remind us that once you set off on a path, even though critics may doubt you, it's OK to believe that there is no CAN'T, WON'T or IMPOSSIBLE. They remind us that it's OK to believe that IMPOSSIBLE IS NOTHING."

- Adidas
  Commercial

Here's an example of an uncomfortable situation:

Your mate has developed a habit of getting up each morning and turning the stereo on loud.

Scaling/Step #2
Attach a score and a word to each feeling

This step involves attaching a score to each of the basic feelings in relation to the situation that is uncomfortable. The number you'll choose will be from 1 to 10. This score provides a means of describing the intensity of your feeling. The words that correspond to this range of numbers are given in the pages that follow.

Notice in the example below that each of the primary emotions have been scaled. This technique will help you to get in touch with feelings that you have trouble accepting or expressing.

Example:

Am I feeling Mad?_(yes)_Intensity?__4__

Am I feeling Glad?_(yes)_ Intensity?__1__

Am I feeling Sad?_(yes)__ Intensity?__2__

Am I feeling Afraid?_(yes)_ Intensity?_1__

Note: When I first ask my clients to scale all four primary emotions, they frequently ask about Glad. For example, it's common for someone who's in a crisis to ask, "What would I feel glad about?" In truth, all four emotions exist and it's important to get in touch with all of them. Although it may be difficult to see at a particular point in time, there are positive aspects to every situation. In the example given, for the person who scales a Mad at

Quote: "Experience taught me a few things. One is to listen to your gut, no matter how good something sounds on paper. The second is that you're generally better off sticking with what you know. And the third is that sometimes your best investments are the ones you don't make."

- Donald Trump

4, a Glad at 1, a Sad at 2 and an Afraid at 1, their reason for assigning a 1 to their Glad could simply be:

"I'm glad my Mad has not overtaken my being."

Even in circumstances that feel dire, the person who's made it to therapy has made a decision to find a solution, they're working toward a goal, and they have every reason to believe that they can resolve their situation. That's worth a Glad of at least 1!

Scaling/Step #3
Try to determine why a score is high

This step involves probing your feeling to determine the reason that you assigned a score.

Mad

When you are mad, you feel angry. The following words help to convey the intensity of this emotion.

How Mad Are You? (Number)	Corresponding Word	Reason You're Mad
1-2	Upset	
3-4	Irritated	
5-6	Angry	
7-8	Irate	
9-10	Rage	

Glad

When you are glad, you're happy. Notice that the words in the following chart describe a range of happiness from a mild "pleased" to a much stronger "ecstatic."

How Glad Are You? (Number)	Corresponding Word	Reason You're Glad
1-2	Pleased	
3-4	Gleeful	
5-6	Excited	
7-8	Thrilled	
9-10	Ecstatic	

Sad

Sadness hurts. It is a feeling that makes us feel powerless or hopeless. Intensity of feeling may be conveyed with words that are weak or strong.

How Sad Are You? (Number)	Corresponding Word	Reason You're Sad
1-2	Down	
3-4	Troubled	
5-6	Hurt	
7-8	Crushed	
9-10	Hopeless	

Afraid

Fear is the belief that the world is unsafe and that security is impossible. Physical clues that often accompany fear include shakiness, a fast heartbeat, tense muscles or a lack of appetite.

How Afraid Are You? (Number)	Corresponding Word	Reason You're Afraid
1-2	Doubtful	
3-4	Anxious	
5-6	Frightened	
7-8	Scared	
9-10	Terrified	

Scaling/Step #4
The conversation

The reason that you unearthed in the previous step becomes the conversation you may need to have. Be sure to read the section on "I Messages" in this chapter to understand Dr. Thomas Gordon's thoughts on how to express your feelings to another person. Although it is possible that your conversation will result in an immediate, positive change, it's also possible or even probable that both parties will need to address underlying emotional issues.

Ideally, the conversation you have will:

- Focus on feelings behind a behavior and not just the behavior

Quote: "You can listen to what everybody says, but the fact remains that you've got to get out there and do the thing yourself."

- Joan Sutherland
  Actress

- Validate each other's feelings (Note: See the section on validation later in this chapter)

- Include non-judgmental suggestions for possible solutions

- Include a discussion about each person's feelings about the optional solutions

Here's how the conversation with a mate who turns the stereo up loud every morning might look:

"I wake up every morning and feel irritated" (focus is on the feelings behind the behavior)

"I know you have a need to listen to music and I know how important this is to you" (validate the other's feelings)

"We need to get some earphones or earplugs" (non-judgmental suggestions for possible solutions)

"I'd rather you get earphones because earplugs bother my ears. Earplugs make my ears feel like they're plugged up with wax" (a discussion about each person's feelings about optional solutions).

Why Scaling Exercises Help

Scaling exercises help us unclog a feeling, nail the intensity and connect with a "why." They help us to deal with our primary emotions when they are at manageable levels. Numbers and words help us to first, determine which emotion we are feeling and second, determine the level of intensity. One of the principle objectives of good communication is to avoid high-intensity anger as much as

Quote: "Listen to the mustn'ts, child. Listen to the don'ts. Listen to the shouldn'ts, the impossibles, the won'ts. Listen to the never haves, then listen close to me... Anything can happen, child. Anything can be."

- Shel Silverstein
  Author

possible. If you're angry, you will be much more open to negotiation at a "level 2" than you are at a "level 10."

Centering

Centering is a technique that I teach my clients when they begin to scale. It's a process of clearing your mind so that you can connect with each emotion. Centering is similar to meditation and it's a skill that I learned in the 1980s when I discovered the work of Dr. Claudia Black. Claudia Black is an author most known for her work with family systems and addictive disorders. She's written over a dozen books for people who have difficulty identifying and expressing their feelings, including *It Will Never Happen to Me, Changing Course* and *Repeat After Me*.

As I've explained in previous chapters, the events of our childhood influence our present beliefs and behaviors. Centering and scaling are both part of a process that involves learning how to own your past and connect it to the present. The goal in all this is to learn new skills that help us to replace old belief systems with new ones.

Being centered means that you are calm, clear and free of stress. In order to reach this state, you will need to take slow, deep breaths. While you inhale, imagine that the energy in your body is stabilizing. As you exhale, see yourself calmly reaching a state of peace and balance.

Meet Jason—
His "Mad" Is
Really an "Afraid"

Note:

In couples counseling, it's important to understand that the fight about where to put the butter is usually not about the butter. More likely, it's about power or control or some issue related to the family of origin.

It is important to note that there's a good chance that when men have high scores for mad, they're really feeling afraid. When women have a high score for sad, they're often feeling mad. In talk therapy, a person's real feeling will usually be revealed if they scale, then talk about their feelings and then scale again. Jason, who came to see me for an explosive temper, is an example. He was arrested and charged with aggravated assault for throwing a picture through a window in his home during an argument with his wife. The court deferred prosecution if he agreed to go to therapy. During his first visit, I asked him how he felt.

> "I'm mad at myself and angry at my girlfriend. She was not charged even though she was part of the fight."

I asked him if he's always had a bad temper.

> "My temper has been a problem since I was a kid and it has cost me three relationships."

During our talk, I explained the concept of primary feelings and asked him to scale.

> Am I feeling Mad?_**(yes)**_Intensity?__**7**__
>
> Am I feeling Glad?_**(no)**_ Intensity?_____
>
> Am I feeling Sad?_**(yes)**__ Intensity?__**1**__
>
> Am I feeling Afraid?_**(yes)**_ Intensity?_**2**__

"I noticed you don't feel glad. All of the primary feelings exist."

> "What would I have to feel glad about?"

Quote: "I realized by the time I turned 30, which happened this year, that I would be going out with girls and they would think I was really funny, but I would know absolutely nothing about them. I decided that's just not the way to go. I have tried to listen more and get to know the person I'm with."

- Matthew Perry
  Actor

"Your glad is probably blocked. Let's talk about the anger you experienced during your childhood."

"I was always worried about behaving like my father. He used to beat up my mother and I was afraid I'd grow up just like him. My parents would fight all the time. When I was little, I'd get in between them so he would not hurt her. My father stopped hitting her when I was big enough to stop him."

I asked Jason to describe how he felt when he was small.

"I was very afraid. I wanted him to stop. I'd hide in my room."

"Jason, when you're arguing with your girlfriend, do you feel afraid?"

"Yes, I'm afraid I'm like my Dad. I'm afraid I might hurt her like he hurt my mother."

"Jason, let's see what happens if you scale again."

Am I feeling Mad?_**(yes)**_Intensity?__**5**__

Am I feeling Glad?_**(yes)**_ Intensity?__**1**__

Am I feeling Sad?_**(yes)**__ Intensity?__**6**__

Am I feeling Afraid?_**(yes)**_ Intensity?_**7**__

"Your scores have changed. Can you explain the change in your feeling?"

"I guess I was more afraid than I realized. I'm not as angry. I understand what is happening. I feel

Quote: "You cannot truly listen to anyone and do anything else at the same time."

- M. Scott Peck
  Author

sad that my mother had to experience my father's anger."

"Many men cover up their fear with anger because they use their anger to control situations. You wanted to control your situation as a child."

"I sure did . . . my Dad was a mean guy."

"You got angry to control your girlfriend. Jason, let's see what happens if you scale again."

Am I feeling Mad?_(yes)_Intensity?__4__

Am I feeling Glad?_(yes)_ Intensity?__3__

Am I feeling Sad?_(yes)_ Intensity?__7__

Am I feeling Afraid?_(yes)_ Intensity?_5__

"Can you explain your scores?"

"My afraid went down because my understanding is up. My glad is up because I realize I can change."

Understanding Transference

Note:
When I first became a counselor, transference was just a word. Thirty years later, it's a funda-mental concept in my psycho-therapy practice.

This might be a good time to review what we said in the chapter about transference. It's important to note that whenever someone overreacts, it's usually due to *transference*.

In Jason's case, it's significant that he used the word *understanding,* because that is the goal. The four pri-mary feelings (Mad, Sad, Glad, Afraid) act as a doorway. They allow us to look at our past and present feelings and make connections so that we understand the reasons behind the intensity of our emotions. Jason was intellec-tually and emotionally blocked. His true feeling was fear and he did not realize that he was *transferring* the fear from his childhood to his girlfriend.

In marriage counseling, there are two avenues to working with couples:

- Transference
- Communication

Although I use both approaches, I find that most of my work is on transference issues. Either one of the individu-als works on transference, or both parties work on their family issues together. I have found that once transfer-ence issues are cleared up, communication improves.

Tool #2: I Messages (Expressing Your Feelings)

Note:
"You" messages communicate blame. We need to unlearn this and take responsibility for ourselves and our feelings.

Once you've used scaling to get in touch with your feelings, "I messages" help you express your feelings to another person. Dr. Thomas Gordon, who introduced "I Messages" in his book, *Parent Effectiveness Training (P.E.T.)*, explains their purpose. He said they help you to express that *"it is I who has the problem and not you."* Your message will either be received without a problem and result in positive change, or the message will trigger a negative reaction in the other person. If this is the case, it will be your turn to non-judgmentally listen and practice Active Listening (See: "Active Listening" later in this chapter). Linda Adams, President of Gordon Training International, explains that there are four types of "I Messages":

Declarative I Messages

The declarative I Message is the simplest form that informs others about your likes and dislikes, feelings, interests and intentions.

The following example builds on Scenario #1 that concerns a husband or boyfriend who accepts a dinner invitation from his mother without talking it over with his significant other. Here are some sample declarative I Messages for his partner:

> "I sometimes enjoy going to your mother's."

> "I'm really upset that plans were made without consulting me."

Responsive I Messages

The responsive I Message may be used when you are asked to do something that you do not want to do. Rather than say yes when you really mean no, a responsive

Quote: "I guess the key is to really listen to what it is you truly need."

- Wynonna Judd
  Entertainer

I Message is an appropriate way to communicate your intention. This form of I Message can contain one or two parts:

Part #1: A Clear Refusal

Examples:

> "I do not want to go."

> "I've decided not to."

A clear statement is preferable to a statement that leaves the door open for further requests.

Examples:

> "I'm busy."

> "I don't have time."

Part #2: An Explanation for Your Refusal

Examples:

> "I do not want to go because I've already made plans."

> "I do not want to go because we already made plans to see *Phantom of the Opera* that day."

Preventative I Messages

This type of I Message may be used when you need to prevent a misunderstanding or enlist help from another person. Two parts include:

Part #1: Statement of Your Needs

Example:

> "I need you to call your parents and explain."

Part #2: The Reason

Example:

> "I need you to call your parents and explain that we already have plans to go to a play."

Confrontational I Messages

This type of I Message may be used when another person's behavior is causing a problem. Three parts include:

Part #1: Begin with the word "when" and use a non-judgmental description of the behavior that is causing a problem.

Example:

> "When you make plans without consulting me."

Part #2: Describe the effect on you.

Example:

> "When you make plans without consulting me, I'm always the one who has had to rearrange my schedule."

Part #3: Include your feelings.

Example:

> "When you make plans without consulting me, I'm always the one who has had to rearrange my schedule and it's very irritating."

Tool #3: Assertive Messages (Expressing Your Feelings)

Note:

An Assertive Message is an "I" message with direction. When I taught Parent Effectiveness Training (PET), I discovered that assertive messages were necessary (especially when I directed treatment centers for delinquent adolescents).

Dr. Thomas Gordon's wife, Linda Adams, is the author of *Effectiveness Training for Women* and *Be Your Best*. While Gordon's I Messages teach people how to deliver messages that foster good communication, her books cover the topic of Assertiveness Messages that are stronger. I Messages contain no consequences. The responsibility of a solution is placed entirely on the other person. Even the confrontive I Message assumes the other person will want to negotiate. I Messages give the other person the benefit of the doubt and they're helpful for highly functioning adults. In contrast, Assertive Messages contain consequences. They're more appropriate when you find yourself repeating the same message over and over. Assertive Messages are I Messages with teeth.

Start With Simple Assertive Messages

If you're uncertain about how your message will be received, start with simple assertive statements much like I Messages and then move to a more confrontational Assertive Message only when necessary.

The following example is an Assertive Message that's been added to a Confrontational I Message:

Part #1 (I Message) Use the word "when" and a non-judgmental description of the problem.

"When you use more than half of the space in the closet"

Part #2 (I Message) Describe the effect on you.

"When you use more than half of the space in the closet, I don't have enough room for my clothes."

Part #3 (I Message) Include your feelings.

"When you use more than half of the space in the closet, I don't have enough room for my clothes and I feel irritated."

Part #4 (Assertive Message) Include a consequence.

"When you use more than half of the space in the closet, I don't have enough room for my clothes and I feel angry. As a result, I would like to discuss how we can solve this problem."

Tips for Using Assertive Messages

Your use of an Assertive Message will be more successful if you:

Use "I" statements instead of "You" statements. You statements imply judgment and blame. In the last example, notice the phrasing in Part #3 of the message:

> "I feel irritated"
>
> instead of
>
> "You make me feel irritated"

Use definitive consequences only when necessary. Although Assertive Messages can include a definitive consequence such as "I will be moving your clothes to the basement," it's best to include the other party in a brainstorming session designed to problem solve.

Tool #4: Validation Tool (a two-in-one tool) Accepting Another's Feelings and Avoiding the Trap of Invalidation

Note:
Validation is something we all need to thrive. It's also something that our society does not teach very well.

Everyone desires validation or a clear expression that our thoughts, words and concerns have value. Validation implies that we accept someone's feelings (happy or sad) or allow them to feel safe about sharing their feelings. Validation does not need to be verbal and can include a nod or a hug.

While validation is the acceptance and acknowledgement of another's feelings, invalidation is the rejection or judgment of someone's feelings. Part of the process of learning to validate involves learning the invalidating remarks that many people think are common or normal.

Validation

When we validate, we communicate that another's feelings are OK and that we accept them.

Simple Validations for Mad

I hear you.

I see the steam coming out of your ears.

I would feel the same way.

You're really angry.

That would make me mad also.

Simple Validations for Glad

Congratulations!

Excellent!

What fun!

Sounds like a real good time.

You sure look happy.

Simple Validations for Sad

I see what you mean.

That sounds like it hurt.

I understand.

You have every reason to be sad.

It's OK.

Simple Validations for Afraid

I'd be afraid too.

That was frightening.

It's real scary.

That's terrifying.

It's OK to be afraid.

Invalidation

Part of learning to validate involves learning to avoid the trap of invalidation. Invalidating remarks tell a person that their feelings are not real. Some invalidations are so habitual that we've been conditioned to think they are normal. Sensitive children who are constantly invalidated by their parents or siblings may be permanently impaired as adults.

Quote: "There is an art of listening. To be able really to listen, one should abandon or put aside all prejudices, preformulations and daily activities . . . But unfortunately most of us listen through a screen of resistance. We are screened with prejudices, whether religious or spiritual, psychological or scientific; or with our daily worries, desires and fears. And with these for a screen, we listen. Therefore, we listen really to our own noise, our own sound, not to what is being said. It is extremely difficult to put aside our training, our prejudices, our inclination, our resistance, and, reaching beyond the verbal expression, to listen so that we understand instantaneously.

> - J. Krishnamurti
> *The First and Last Freedom*

Invalidations for Mad

You're making a big deal out of nothing.

You should be happy.

It can't be that bad.

Get over it.

You're just tired.

Invalidations for Glad

Stop laughing.

Don't look so pleased with yourself.

Don't get too happy.

It's not going to last.

If you're too happy, your lows will be lower.

Invalidations for Sad

Cheer up.

Don't cry.

I'm sure she means well.

Everything happens for a reason.

You are a cry baby.

Quote: "Reexamine all that you have been told... dismiss that which insults your soul."

- Walt Whitman
  Poet

Invalidations for Afraid

You are making a big deal out of nothing.

What's wrong with you?

You're not being rational.

You're a worry wart.

You're a big baby.

Tool #5: Active Listening (Becoming a Better Listener)

Note:
Active Listening is important because it teaches us to facilitate someone else's growth. The by-product is understanding the other person's point of view and the result can be true intimacy.

A step-by-step approach to listening can often bring out very deep feelings. Listening is not the same as understanding. Listening exercises can help us become better listeners but the real key to better communication is understanding. We all need to understand and be understood—particularly in the context of a personal relationship. Listening leads to better understanding.

How often do you know what your partner (or someone you work with) thinks or feels? Does he/she understand what you are thinking or feeling? Active listening is a tool to help us to understand others and to help them understand us.

Paraphrasing

Paraphrasing a speaker's statement helps us understand how much we *pay attention*. Here's how it works:

Step #1 Schedule some time
Schedule some time with your partner and plan to take turns speaking.

Step #2 Select topics and echo your partner
Each partner should select a topic that is not emotionally charged. Echoing sets up a condition for partners to explore feelings. You create a sounding board that provides increased understanding for both parties.

Quote: "My entire life has been an attempt to get back to the kind of feelings you have on a field. The sense of brother-hood, the esprit de corps, the focus -- there being no past or future, just the ball. As trite as it sounds, I was happiest playing ball."

- David Duchovny
  Actor

Sample Scenario/Exercise

The following exercise is an example of what I rehearse with patients in a session with the suggestion that they repeat it at home. I explain that it's the concept that's important and that they can invent their own phrases. If the experience is positive, there is a good possibility that they will repeat it.

Statement
One person begins by stating their topic aloud. Example:

> "We're supposed to go to my mother's on Sunday night but I don't want to go."

Paraphrase
In response, the other party repeats what they heard using different words.

> "You don't want to go to your Mom's on Sunday night."

The joke about therapists saying, "Uh Huh..." in a session is based on a partial truth. It's more than an "Uh Huh...." It's really a form of paraphrasing called *reflective statements*. By repeating aloud what you've heard, you echo back what's said to make sure you understand. Helen Keller said, "I do not want the peace which passeth understanding, I want the understanding which bringeth peace."

Meet Joan and Fred

Note:

Two things that I find astounding about humans include:

- *Our ability to stay stagnant and thwart learning*

- *When we have the need and we're shown the way, we have a unique ability to learn other ways of being.*

When two people are in an argument, it is common for both parties to respond to what they *think* the other party said. If either party forms a response based on a false impression, the argument can spiral out of control.

Fred and Joan's Fight

Fred and Joan's argument over Fred's decision to buy a truck is an example. Here's a description of the conflict that has existed for six months:

Although Fred and Joan have limited funds:

- Fred wants to purchase a truck that is powerful enough to pull his boat.

- Joan prefers that they build a playroom in the basement.

- Fred thinks the kids have room to play in their bedrooms and feels that his wife babies their children.

- Joan assumes that he's selfish and that he wants to keep up with their neighbor next door.

- Fred feels that he provides his family with a good life and that he deserves to buy a new truck with the money he's earned from working overtime.

- Joan feels that he's always putting his fishing friends ahead of his family.

Quote: "You'll never find peace of mind until you listen to your heart."

- George Michael
  Musician

When Fred and Joan started counseling, they began to work on their communication. They'll use paraphrasing in a session while they talk about how to spend their money. Whenever one of the partner's speaks, the other partner is required to repeat the essence of what he/she said. I'm the referee and I ask Joan to start:

[Joan] "I want a place for the kid's toys because he gets mad when he comes home and their toys are all over the place."

[Fred] "They always get what they want and you don't want me to buy the truck."

[Joan] "No, that's not what I meant."

[Guy] "Joan, repeat what you said."

[Joan] "He always gets mad when he sees toys in the living room. A playroom would provide a solution and I would not have to work so hard."

[Fred] "A playroom would mean you would not work so hard because the toys would not be spread all over the living room."

[Joan] "Yes, that's what I said."

[Guy] "Fred, now it's your turn."

[Fred] "I think the kids always get what they want. You should teach the kids to pick up their toys before I come home."

Quote: "Manners are a sensitive awareness of the feelings of others. If you have that awareness, you have good manners, no matter what fork you use."

- Emily Post
*Etiquette in Society,
in Business, in
Politics and at Home*

[Joan] "You just don't want to spend your money on a playroom."

[Fred] "That's not what I said."

[Guy] "Joan, repeat what you think Fred said."

[Joan] "He thinks the kids are spoiled and I'm not training them to be responsible."

[Fred] "Yes, that's what I said."

At this point, Fred and Joan have not reached agreement but they're starting to listen to each other. They're clearer on their disagreement. Paraphrasing helps to make sure they don't mind read. Next, comes the negotiation. By now, they know they each need to rephrase what the other person says. After each party paraphrases what their partner said, they'll need feedback about whether they're right or wrong.

[Guy] "Joan, it's now your turn."

[Joan] "I really think the playroom is more important than the truck."

[Fred] "She feels the playroom is more important than my need to have a new truck."

[Joan] "We have a real problem because there's only so much money and the kids need a place to horse around where they won't break anything."

[Fred] "She believes the kids need a place to be kids and not be restrained by furniture."

[Joan] "Yes, that's right."

[Fred] "I feel that it's important for me to own a truck that can pull my fishing boat so I can go fishing."

[Joan] "You never take the kids fishing."

[Fred] "That's not what I said but this is important enough that I will take them."

[Joan] "You feel if you owned a new truck, you'd take the kids fishing."

[Fred] "Yes, that's right."

[Joan] "How can we resolve this?"

[Fred] "I feel frustrated that we have not found a solution but we're not yelling and screaming like we usually do."

[Joan] "How can we both get what we want?"

After two sessions of negotiations, Fred and Joan decided that they would buy a used truck. With the money that they saved and with the help of his fishing buddies, Fred decided to fix up the basement, and has also agreed to take the kids fishing with him at least once a month. Joan has also agreed to get the kids to confine their toys to the basement.

Quote: "One looks back with appreciation to the brilliant teachers, but with gratitude to those who touched our human feelings. The curriculum is so much necessary raw material, but warmth is the vital element for the growing plant and for the soul of the child."

> - Carl G. Jung
>   Analytical
>   Psychologist

Tips on Listening

Listening involves many nuances. Here are some examples:

Focus on the Other Person's Feelings

Listen to the content of what the other person is saying but try to focus (and identify) his/her underlying feelings.

Give the Other Person Your Full Attention

Don't be engaged in any task when the other person is talking about their feelings (this includes mentally preparing a response while he/she is speaking). Try to use eye contact as much as possible.

Don't Interrupt

Try to monitor whether you interrupt other people or jump to conclusions.

Use Validation

Validating remarks can help you show understanding. Examples include:

"I understand."

"I see."

Practice Paraphrasing

Paraphrasing shows that you have a desire to confirm exactly what the speaker is saying. Examples include:

"It sounds as if_____."

"You sound angry about____."

Quote: "I think one's feelings waste themselves in words; they ought all to be distilled into actions which bring results."

- Florence Nightingale
  Radical Innovator,
  Nursing Care

"I hear you saying that_____."

"So you felt_____."

Tool #6: Time Out (When Feelings Erupt)

Note:
Time Outs give couples relief from an intense struggle, but more importantly, it gives a person time to face himself/herself and come to grips with his/her role in the conflict.

A time out is designed to create space when a conflict occurs, allowing both parties time to reflect on their feelings. If used correctly, a time out can prevent a conflict from escalating and facilitate reconnection.

Pre-Agreement to Calm Down

A Time Out is a coping tool when you feel tempers are about to flare. It's a pre-agreed upon plan to calm down, cool off and look within.

Steps for Creating a Time Out

Use the following steps as guidelines to customize a Time Out technique that suits you.

Time Out/Step #1
Setting up your time out agreement
Setting up a time out agreement requires some advance planning before it can be implemented. Here are the essential points that form the basis of the agreement:

- When problems arise, you will look for patterns of behavior that lead up to a conflict.

- Invent a verbal or nonverbal signal that indicates a time out is needed.

- Agree on the length of a time out (20 minutes to 24 hours).

- During the time out, each party will use the time to look within and connect to feelings that arose when the conflict started, deeper feelings that may have been difficult to identify or childhood memories that may have been triggered.

Quote: "The most difficult thing in any negotiation, almost, is making sure that you strip it of the emotion and deal with the facts."

- Howard Baker
  United States
  Ambassador
  to Japan

Time Out/Step #2
Calling a time out

When trouble arises, one of the partners calls a time out and both parties take an agreed upon time break. During the break, each party uses the time to look within and gather answers to the agreed upon questions. After the break, the parties reconnect and share answers to each of their questions.

Communication Skills Can Help Resolve Any Type of Conflict

Note:
The key to effective communication is understanding.

The communication skills covered in this chapter have proven to be effective strategies for couples, and the same skills can easily be used to facilitate nonviolent solutions to conflicts between nations.

In April 2005, I was asked to contribute an article to a publication called *The Commonwealth Tree*. Each issue has a theme and the April paper focused on conflict and conflict resolution—in the media, in our communities, in politics and between one another. My article contained a description of the tools contained in this chapter (scaling, I messages, validation and paraphrasing) These techniques help in the process of conflict resolution regardless of the circumstances.

The Commonwealth Tree (www.commonwealthtree.org) is a small publication that's based in southern Wisconsin. Dave Haldiman, who's the editor and publisher, launched the paper as a public space where people can meet, learn about one another and share their ideas. As he says, "Our future is created by the lives we live now. It comes from how we examine our beliefs, consider the beliefs of others, and how we choose to act in our communities."

Publications like *The Commonwealth Tree* help us to remember that we have alternatives—in this case, alternative media. The major media is so large, we rarely hear good news. For example, Congressional Representative Dennis Kucinich's proposal for a Department of Peace contains a plan for a cutting-edge resource for ideas about conflict resolution, yet this initiative has not yet made national news. At the present time, the bill has 61 cosponsors and highlights from the legislation include:

Quote: "Mankind are governed more by their feelings than by reason."

- Samuel Adams Founding Father, Signer of the Declaration of Independence and cousin to John Adams, President of the United States

- Reduce domestic and international violence

- Provide assistance for the efforts of city, county and state governments in coordinating existing programs in their own communities, as well as newly developed programs by the Department of Peace

- Teach violence prevention and mediation to America's school children

- Treat and dismantle gang psychology

- Rehabilitate the prison population

- Build peacemaking efforts among conflicting cultures both here and abroad

- Support our military with complementary approaches to ending violence

- Gather and coordinate information and recommendations from America's peace community

- Create and administer a United States Peace Academy, acting as a sister organization to the United States Military Academy

Dennis Kucinich and others who proposed a Department of Peace explain that current policy-making tends toward reactive, not proactive approaches to violence reduction. Walter Cronkite called a Department of Peace, "a massive but basic change in our culture, in our entire approach to relationships to other human beings." For more details, visit www.thepeacealliance.org.

Chapter 8

RULE #8

By Focusing on Yourself— You Focus on What You Can Control

Trying to control another person is a waste of time because ultimately we all have free will

"As I worked with people over the years, I realized how frequently people blame others for their situation. If I were only able to teach one concept to patients—I would tell them that we are in charge of our own happiness."

Human Beings and Control

When a person tries to control another human being, it's usually to satisfy his/her own wants or needs. The story of Wanda Holloway, Houston's "Cheerleader Mom," is a classic example. In 1991, Wanda was convicted of trying to hire a hit man to kill Verna Heath, the mother of her daughter's cheerleader rival. Wanda hoped Heath's daughter would become so upset she would quit the cheerleading squad, opening up a position for Holloway's daughter Shanna.

Power and Control

Most people do not like to accept the idea that they have no control over others. Human beings, particularly in Western society, are driven to control events (and sometimes people) in their everyday lives. Imposing one's will on the world or controlling one's environment to suit one's own needs is a Western obsession. In contrast, the Eastern view sees control as an illusion, mostly because of the mystical idea that all life is one.

Scientific research tends to support the need for *some* control and it has been shown to be an intrinsic necessity of life. Several international studies link chronic stress to a lack of control. Examples include:

The Volvo Study

Boredom in daily routine and time demands at work are the result of low personal control in the workplace. Both have been shown to cause stress. In a well-known study that took place in Sweden in a Volvo car plant, researchers observed that workers who produced cars on the production line experienced a lot of dissatisfaction with

Quote: "It isn't until you come to a spiritual understanding of who you are—not necessarily a religious feeling, but deep down, the spirit within—that you can begin to take control."

- Oprah Winfrey

their job. The job consisted of having to complete repetitive tasks under the pressure of a deadline. The result was frequent absenteeism, elevated blood pressure, and job dissatisfaction.

When Volvo reorganized the work schedule into teams with flexible work roles and the ability to swap jobs, job satisfaction increased, blood pressure decreased and the workers reported a greater sense of well-being.

Swedish Commuters

Researchers who studied the behavior of Swedish commuters found that those who had control over choices, such as location of seating and decisions with whom to sit, experienced less stress. Simple, predictable occurrences make us feel as though we are in control.

In Western society, the concept of power is associated with the ability to control. A large amount of control implies great strength and a small amount of control implies weakness. Equating control with strength ignores the element of cooperation that is necessary for control. Without cooperation, control is an illusion. People *give control* to bosses, governments, religions, groups and individuals. In addition, human beings cooperate for different reasons:

- Fear or obligation

- Love or respect

- Coercion or intimidation

- Manipulation or lie

Quote: "We cannot always control our thoughts, but we can control our words, and repetition impresses the subconscious, and we are then master of the situation."

- Jane Fonda

Ultimately, we control only our own thoughts and actions (that is, if we're diligently aware and we work very hard). The issue of control involves choices and all choices have consequences.

"Is that outfit on Mom's approved list?"

The Controlling Parent

Note:
When you're working with children and adolescents, it's important to provide structure as well as good choices.

Acontrolling parent who becomes enmeshed in his/her child's life is trying to vicariously fill his/her own unmet needs. They are convinced that their own life will be better if their child is successful according to their own definition of success.

Reasons Why a Parent May Try to Control a Child

There are numerous reasons a parent may try to control a child:

- As a young person, the parent's emotional needs were not met. This may be due to alcohol, drugs, compulsive behavior, arguing or extreme rigid behavior.

- Having received very little security in childhood, they have a desperate need to control other people.

- They dream about how things "could be."

- By focusing on someone else (such as a child), they avoid taking responsibility for themselves.

Cooperation Through Mutual Benefit

The very best form of cooperation is based on mutual benefit. Regardless of whether you are dealing with a child or an adult, it is important to understand that:

- All human beings have a free will.

- Human beings are responsible for their own actions.

- Everyone controls only himself or herself according to an agreement.

- Mature people live up to promises that they have made.

Meet Josh

Note:
Crossroads' day treatment program for children and adolescents has been amazingly successful. It provides structure, opportunity for realistic self-evaluation, positive reinforcement for change, family and community support and change. It also provides in-home family therapy.

Each person's motivations are tied to benefits that are exchanged. This strategy teaches us to carefully examine our options before making choices.

Children and young adults are usually motivated by external rewards. Josh, a 16-year-old patient who spent six months in the day program at Crossroads[1] is an example. Josh's father had a drug and alcohol problem and was killed in a car accident when he was very young. His codependent mother remarried and died of cancer when Josh was a young teenager. Fortunately, Bill, Josh's stepfather is an extremely good parent. When I met Josh, he was diagnosed as a budding schizophrenic and had been caught stealing hip-hop jewelry. He had started the day program at Crossroads that's designed for hard-to-reach youths and like many young people in the day program, Josh was very uncooperative. He would not talk and he would often skip his medication. Shortly after he joined the program, the day staff identified three behavior goals for Josh:

- Stop stealing

- Take medication

- Participate (by talking) in group sessions

---

[1] Children's and Adolescent's Day Treatment Program – a program designed to provide intensive counseling in a weekly structured setting. Participants meet Monday through Friday for four hours a day and the family meets once-a-week for two hours. Details are available at www.crossroads73.com/programs.

To get Josh to cooperate, the day team looked for something that Josh wanted. Because he had been caught stealing hip-hop jewelry, it was very likely that he would want more—but he needed *money*. Susan and Rick, who run the day program, invented a very clever proposal they planned to present to Bill, Josh's stepfather. They would ask Bill to *pay* Josh to cooperate for a minimum of two months. In exchange for specific tasks that the staff needed from Josh, he would earn money he could use to buy jewelry.

Action	Payment
Talk for five minutes in a group session.	$2
Take medication	$2

At first, Josh's stepfather Bill was reluctant:

"Shouldn't Josh know that stealing is wrong?
Are you asking me to bribe Josh?"

In truth, most people will cooperate with an understanding of some future benefit. And that benefit is often money. Money that is offered as a reward is not bribery. The dictionary provides the following definitions:

Tip: Parents who give rewards before positive behavior are rarely successful.

Reward	Bribe
Dictionary.com: Something given or received in recompense for worthy behavior. The return for performance of a desired behavior.	**Webster's Dictionary:** To pervert judgment or corrupt the action of a person in a position of trust, by some gift or promise.
A *reward* is given after positive behavior.	A *bribe* is given in exchange for negative behavior.

Bill still did not see the benefit of paying Josh, but he agreed to the staff's proposal because he did not know what else to do.

Next, the day staff talked to Josh about the agreement. Josh responded positively to the idea and he kept his part of the deal by talking in group sessions and taking his medication. At the end of six months, Josh no longer needed the money he earned through the agreement with Bill. Josh realized the benefits of participating in group sessions and saw that the medication had helped him. He was now internally motivated. Eventually, the staff helped Josh get a job where he functioned as an adult and earned a paycheck instead of payments from Bill.

Setting Up a Behavior Program

Note:
Have you ever noticed that adults are always paid on Fridays and never on Mondays? That's because payment after a behavior is considered to be a form of reinforcement.

As a parent, once you say, "I'll make you do [some task]," you're headed for trouble. Asking the question, "How can I help you get what you want?" will facilitate the cooperation that a parent (or anyone in a position of authority) needs from a child. Examples include:

Agrees To:	In Exchange for:
Complete homework	Time on the family computer
Clean up bedroom	Phone calls with a boyfriend or girlfriend
Take a younger brother or sister to [meeting or activity]	Money

Many parents understand the art of parent negotiations. My neighbor George is an example. While talking to his 13-year-old son about homework he said,

"Would you do your homework for a million dollars?"

His son, who likes TV a lot more than homework said,

"Yeah!"

His father, now in negotiating mode, said,

"Would you do your homework for $10,000?"

Quote: "There are two big forces at work, external and internal. We have very little control over external forces such as tornadoes, earthquakes, floods, disasters, illness and pain. What really matters is the internal force. How do I respond to those disasters? Over that I have complete control."

- Leo Buscaglia
   Author

His son answered,

"Yes!"

George, who had already decided to pay a small sum to his son as a reward for doing homework said,

"OK . . . now we're working on the price . . ."

In the final round of father-son negotiations, George agreed to pay:

Action	Payment
Homework completed before 7:00 p.m.	$3 per day
Homework completed before 9:00 p.m.	$2 per day

Meet Jane

A person who is in an unsatisfactory relationship often feels that he/she is stuck. The focus is often on the changes a "partner can make." Here's what he/she frequently overlooks:

- Everyone is in control of their own experiences and not the experiences of another person.

- People who accept an unsatisfactory circumstance have often lost contact with their intuition or inner reality.

- It's impossible to look to someone else to make you happy.

- Your intuition is the source of your creativity and imagination. By getting in touch with this side of yourself you can create positive changes in your life.

Jane, who came to see me after ten years in an unsatisfactory marriage, is a classic example of someone who feels that she is stuck because she cannot control another person. Jane's husband plays sports five nights a week and in response, Jane sits at home feeling depressed. She started therapy to learn how she could get her husband to stay home and get him into therapy. As she explained:

> "I have tried everything I can think of to get my husband to be a family man and spend more time at home. Nothing works—he's still playing sports five nights a week."

Quote: "Concern should drive us into action and not into a depression. No man is free who cannot control himself."

- Pythagoras

When I asked her what she did to try to control her husband, she said,

> "I have cooked good meals, I tried to get him interested in going to plays, I have threatened to leave and I had two children thinking that he would be interested in being a father. I also tried to join him at his sporting events but he won't reciprocate by joining me and the kids."

Like many people, Jane believes that she can control her spouse. She feels that it's a matter of learning how. When we began to talk about the things in Jane's life that she could control, it became clear that her husband was not among them. Instead of focusing on how to control her husband, I asked Jane what would make her happy. Her answer had nothing to do with her husband:

> "I would like to get a better job. I've always wanted to be an accountant. I'm very good with numbers."

Because Jane was alone a lot, we talked over the possibility of classes that would help her earn a degree in accounting. Jane started school six months later. She also started going to plays with a girlfriend and later joined a theater group. Jane earned a degree within two years and decided to leave her husband, who would not work on his addiction to sports. Jane felt happy—she had found a new job and was looking forward to finding someone with similar interests.

Detective Work: How Enmeshed Are You?

Note:
Enmeshment is "stuck-together-ness" that exists in dysfunctional families. In psychotherapy, the state of being "stuck" is called an "undifferentiated ego mass" that's due to an incomplete "sense of self."

S ay the word "enmeshed" and your brain should provide the meaning. If nothing comes to mind, here's a definition from the dictionary:

> " To catch or involve someone in something unpleasant or dangerous from which it is difficult to escape"

This exercise is designed to help you determine if you're overly enmeshed with another person. When a person is overly enmeshed, they need to detach from the person in their life who they try to control so that they can focus on their own life.

Imagine that you're the person who is in the scenario that's described. Read each of the situations to determine if you understand which of the choices represent extreme enmeshment:

Scenario 1: Your Significant Other Leaves Town

Your significant other leaves town on a business trip. Would you:

a. Clean, cook meals and go to a movie while he/she is away?

b. Stay in bed, watch TV, order a pizza and call 3-4 friends just to talk?

c. Sit around the house, feel too upset to eat and call your significant other on his/her cell phone until they get home?

Quote: "John Travolta said
he sometimes lets his friends
take control of his airplane even
though they don't know what
they're doing. Then Travolta
said he often does the same
thing with his career."

- Conan O'Brien

d. Theaten to kill yourself just before he/she leaves, take pills and be rushed to the hospital because of an overdose—forcing him/her to stay home.

Scenario 2: Your Significant Other Plans a Hike

While you're on vacation with your in-laws, your significant other decides he/she would like to take a hike with his/her father. Would you:

a. Applaud the idea and see it as a chance for your significant other to spend some time alone with his/her parent?

b. Resent that he/she is planning a hike without you?

c. Threaten to breakup or divorce him/her if he/she goes on the hike?

d. Slit your wrists if he/she goes on the hike?

Scenario 3: Your Children Are Invited to Stay Overnight

Your two children have grown up to be preteenagers and they have an invitation to stay overnight at a friend's house. You know the family and you know they will be safe. Would you:

a. Call the mother and see what they have planned?

b. Invite the other family's children overnight to see if things go well before allowing your two children to stay overnight?

Quote: "I cannot always control what goes on outside. But I can always control what goes on inside."

- Wayne Dyer
  Author

c. Tell your children that even though they've known their friends for a long time, it's not possible to ever trust anyone—and tell them they must stay home?

d. Let them go but make an excuse to go over to the house.

The Answers

In each of the scenarios, choices c and d are the most extreme examples of enmeshment.

Parental Narcissism 101

Notes

Chapter 9

RULE #9

Good Growth or Change Often Follows What Is Perceived to Be Bad

Have you ever heard the expression:
There's light at the end of the tunnel? Or, it's always dark before the dawn?

"Looking back over the crises in my own life, I like to compare it to the stock market—always trending up [hopefully] but having a lot of ups and downs. And when I look at the downs—I realize that they represented important opportunities for significant change."

The Duality of Experience

Note:
When circumstances look dark, it's time to dig deep and fig-ure out what you need to fix. I consider pain to be my friend because it tells me that there is something wrong.

Did you ever notice that the suspense build-up in many movies occurs at night? As the dawn breaks, there's usually a shift and what was perceived as horrible agony is restored to normal.

In a movie, as in life, the conflict, or the tension that intensifies to a crisis, pushes a film's char-acters toward a resolution—until equilibrium is restored. The point at which a conflict is resolved is called a climax and it's at this juncture that a character usually experiences a change in the form of intellectual, emotional or spiritual growth. In the field of psychotherapy, this is called a *corrective emotional experience*.

When Circumstances Look Dark

When you're in midst of a test or trial, you will undoubt-edly find that it is difficult to have positive thoughts. Emotions tend to flood a person's perspective and over-whelm the intellect. When a situation looks dark, it's imperative that your intellect win this battle because your thoughts about your situation will be one of the secrets to your recovery. For example, it is important to remind yourself that pain is your best friend. Pain represents an opportunity to grow. Keep in mind:

- Circumstances that appear dark may simply be a cata-lyst that's required to help you find a healthier path.

- Life's rigorous hurdles allow you to discover who you are and what makes you happy.

Quote: "Necessity is the mother of invention."

- Anonymous

Don't Stay in Free Fall

Many people freeze when life takes an unexpected turn, and this typically has negative results. If you've been able to train your thoughts, the next phase will require you to become an inventor. Many people have heard the expression "back to the drawing board." For an inventor who works on sketches, this means starting over from scratch. When an inventor "returns to the drawing board" he clears his desk and begins with a blank piece of paper. He/she will get rid of the old to make way for the new. In your life, you'll need to put away traces of your old life in order to make room for something new.

Preparing for change is essential, and remaining attached to the remnants of your old life or old patterns will delay your progress. Native American shamans understand this principle. In *Secrets of Shamanism*, authors Jose and Lena Stevens explain, "every shaman knows that in order to create something new, something first must be destroyed. The old form is taken apart and from its energetic source, something new arises. Shamanically speaking, all creating is based on some form of destruction. Shamans are comfortable with destruction and have learned not to fear it because without it they know there can be no life."

The idea that destruction must precede new growth is reflected in nature in the change of seasons. Plant life dies in the fall and winter and the plants are replaced by new growth each spring.

To avoid the free fall that often locks a person into a stagnant pattern:

Take steps to clear traces of your old life and old patterns. Clean out the rooms in your house or apartment, rearrange the furniture, adopt new habits and explore areas of the city you've never explored before. Look for ways to break up your routines. Become an "agent" of change.

Detach from activities or people who may be blocking change. The people in your life or your weekly activities may be keeping you in a holding pattern or distracting you from the necessary steps that are needed to change.

"They say there's darkness before the dawn, but this is ridiculous."

Meet Richard

Every experience has a positive and negative side and it's usually the negative experiences that we remember the most. In spite of powerful negative memories of life's harsh events, there are often positive outcomes to every experience. The people I counsel often can't see positive outcomes until their crisis is over. It's at that point that they begin to see growth and positive change. Richard, age 25, came to see me when he was going through a divorce. His wife, whom he loved, had left him for another man and he was in tremendous pain. During their life together, Richard did all the housework and all the cooking.

> "My wife was very beautiful looking. She was tall and slim and she made heads turn wherever we went. I'm not at all that good looking and I'm overweight. I felt grateful to be married to such a stunning woman. She looked like a model and it helped my ego."

I asked Richard to tell me about his wife.

> "She did have a high opinion of herself. I guess you could call it conceit. She always received a lot of attention. She probably grew tired of me. I've cried a lot and I've had trouble sleeping."

After many weeks of looking at himself, Richard started to accept who he was and the positive aspects of his life. He realized he was a talented cook and a caring human being.

Quote: "If you're going through hell, keep going."

- Sir Winston Churchill

As Richard began to feel self-assured, he started to believe that he was an attractive person. Fortunately, he has a good family support system. His family reinforced everything Richard and I talked about in our counseling sessions.

Richard's parents not only supported him but he also noticed that he had an unusual amount of support from his ex in-laws. They told him they had a better relationship with him than they did with their daughter. Months later, he was past his crisis and was starting to experience growth.

One day, he came in smiling and looking one thousand pounds lighter.

"It was my fault." He said.

"What was your fault?" I asked.

"I married my wife for the wrong reasons. I did it entirely for my self-esteem. I picked a superficial woman because she was 'arm candy.' I thought a beautiful looking wife would make up for all the years I was teased about my weight—all those cruel comments by the kids in school."

"It's only been recently that I've started to see my good points. As I began to work on things about myself I didn't like, I started to work out and several pounds came off. My whole life has changed. I signed up for college classes and I've also reconnected with friends I did not see while I was married.'

Quote: "They always say that time changes things, but you actually have to change them yourself."

- Andy Warhol
    American Pop Artist

Two years after his divorce, Richard met and married a very caring woman who appreciated his talents, as he himself now did. His life had changed drastically and he recognized that his divorce had brought great pain but a new life had grown out of a traumatic experience. He felt so positive, he wrote to his ex-wife and thanked her.

"Our therapist says good growth always follows what appears to be bad. We just fired him."

Stepping Out of the Box

Note:
When we're in pain, it forces us to "step outside the box" to find creative and innovative ways to grow.

If you've successfully made preparations for change by cleaning out the old to make room for the new, you will be ready to "step out of the box." At this point, you will need to:

Go Inward
Going inward means exploring what makes you happy.

Go Outward
Going outward means moving among new people and groups to make the connections you need to invent a new future.

Make these your goals, but be kind to yourself. Don't expect to accomplish these steps overnight. To illustrate how I learned the necessity of these steps in this order, I'd like to relay a story from my own life.

Like a lot of young people, I was pushed (or nudged) in a career direction that did not evolve from an inward search. My family encouraged me to take business courses in college and I followed their advice. However, I took psychology courses as electives. Those electives made my college experience very enjoyable. After graduating with a Bachelors in Business Administration, I started graduate work in an MBA program. The psychology electives were no longer available, and I realized that I did not like my major. It was during my second semester, while I was seeing a psychotherapist, that I discovered counseling. I remember saying to my counselor, "I'd be really good at what you're doing," and she agreed. I was faced with an important decision. I could either continue my studies on a career path to please my family or switch into the Masters program for Counseling and Guidance, a field I

Quote: "First they ignore you, then they laugh at you, then they fight you, then you win."

-Mahatma Gandhi

discovered that I loved. To make this decision, I had to think carefully about what made me happy, and to do this I had to "go inside."

Although I knew I had found my niche, I faced another work-related challenge in 1972 when I graduated from school. Wisconsin was in a deep recession and there were no jobs available for graduates in the Masters program. Rather than take a low-paying job that I did not like, I volunteered for a practicum at Whitewater University. The practicum broadened my counseling experience and connected me with people who later became my partners when I founded Crossroads.

Volunteering for a practicum is an example of what I mean by "going outward." Once you discover what it is that you like, volunteer work is one example of a step you can take to make connections on a new path.

Inventors Know About "Trial and Error"

Note:
When I founded Crossroads, I thought it would be a project that would only last five years. That was thirty years ago and the mental health counseling work I've done has been one of my life's most cherished and challenging experiences. I'm thankful for the 1972 recession and the fact that I could not find a job.

All inventors know there may be many trips back to the drawing board. Famous inventors such as Thomas Edison had many inventions but he's famous for only one or two. When you're reinventing and "going outward," don't get discouraged by trial and error. Inventors often say that they learn more from their failures than they do from their successes. Here are some examples of activities that will help you go outward:

Volunteer Work
Making connections as a volunteer is often how people find work that they love.

Classes
Continuing education is one of the most popular ways for people to explore new ideas and skills.

Reading
Challenge yourself weekly by scanning the magazine section in the local library or bookstore. Pick up ten popular magazines. Open one and start by reading the table of contents. Look for informative articles that help you think about yourself and your new life.

Vocational Testing
Schools frequently offer vocational testing. Call local colleges and inquire about tests.

Ten Rules for Being Human

Note:
Dr. Cherie Carter-Scott's book is full of anecdotes drawn from stories about her family, close friends, and workshop participants.

Dr. Cherie Carter-Scott's "Ten Rules for Being Human" is a poem that later evolved into a book called *If Life Is A Game, These Are the Rules*:

Ten Rules For Being Human
by Dr. Cherie Carter-Scott

1. You will receive a body. You may like it or hate it, but it will be yours for the entire period this time around.

2. You will learn lessons. You are enrolled in a full-time informal school called "Life." Each day in this school you will have the opportunity to learn lessons. You may like the lessons or think them irrelevant or stupid.

3. There are no mistakes, only lessons. Growth is a process of trial and error, experimentation. The "failed" experiments are as much a part of the process as the experiment that ultimately "works."

4. A lesson is repeated until it is learned. A lesson will be presented to you in various forms until you have learned it. When you have learned it, you can go on to the next lesson.

5. Learning lessons does not end. There is no part of life that does not contain its lessons. If you are alive, there are lessons to be learned.

6. "There" is no better than "here." When your "there" has become a "here," you will simply obtain another "there" that will, again, look better than "here."

Quote: "All the adversity I've had in my life, all my troubles and obstacles, have strengthened me... You may not realize it when it happens, but a kick in the teeth may be the best thing in the world for you. "

— Walt Disney

7. Others are merely mirrors of you. You cannot love or hate something about another person unless it reflects something you love or hate about yourself.

8. What you make of your life is up to you. You have all the tools and resources you need. What you do with them is up to you. The choice is yours.

9. The answers to life's questions lie inside you. All you need to do is look, listen, and trust.

10. You will forget all this.

Chapter 10

RULE #10

When You Let Your Mind Override What Your Gut Is Telling You, the Decision Will Cost You

Trust Your Gut.

"The major mistakes I've made in my life have caused me a lot of pain. When I thought about my experiences, I remembered that my gut said, 'no' but my narcissistic ego said 'you'll make it work.' We usually pay heavy dues when we don't listen to our intuition."

The Science Behind Your Feelings

Note:
Eighty to ninety percent of the work that I do involves getting people to get in touch with their "gut," or intuition. It involves a lot of "unlearning."

Scientists refer to our gut as a "second brain" because at a cellular level, the neurons in the enteric (gut) system use the same building blocks as our brain. The idea that our gut functions as a second brain lends weight to the fact that there is a biological basis for what is commonly called a "gut reaction." In his book *The Second Brain*, Dr. Michael Gershon describes the sophisticated neurological controls located in our digestive tract.

Dense Clusters of Peptides in the Emotional Centers

Neuropharmacologists and psychiatrists at Johns Hopkins University are credited with a discovery that is an important part of this story. A team that included a female neuroscientist named Candace Pert found what are called opiate receptors in the brain. Interestingly, there is a very dense network of similar receptors in the gut.

A Physical Network That Stores Emotions

A receptor is a tiny dock on a molecule that locks on to another molecule somewhat like a ship that docks on a space station in a sci fi novel. Millions of receptors are attached to cells all over our bodies, and the locking mechanism is the basis for molecular interaction in every system. Opiates belong to a class of proteins called *peptides* and they're one of several other proteins that regulate our behavior, our moods and our health. Besides opiates, other peptides that regulate behavior include seratonin, endorphins and epinephrine (commonly called adrenaline). This means that there is a physical network that stores emotional memories all throughout the body—particularly in the area of the stomach. Scientists are only beginning to uncover interesting relationships between the

Quote: "Denial ain't just a river in Egypt."

- Mark Twain

nervous system and the body. For example, it is known that the flow of peptides may be altered with deep breathing similar to the breathing that is recommended in meditation and yoga.

Michael Ruff, Candace Pert's husband, has discovered a link between our immune system's macrophage cells and neuropeptides. The receptors on macrophages accomodate every neuropeptide, implying that there is a connection between our emotional state and our health. Viruses in our bodies can lock on to the receptor sites used by the body's neuropeptides. If those sites are occupied by neuropeptides, viruses can't lock on. Michael Ruff and Candace Pert believe that this explains why depressed people get sick more often than people who are not depressed.

Meet Carla

Many characters in movies teach us to trust our intuition. By listening and trusting their gut, they have a liberating vision. Examples include Neo, who sees *The Matrix* for what it is, *Star Wars'* Luke Skywalker, who decides to trust the "force," and Truman Burbank, who follows his hunch and decides to explore the edge of the set in *The Truman Show.*

It's when we don't trust our gut that we get into trouble, and the dues are usually heavy. Nearly every divorced person whom I've counseled will admit that they wished they had listened to their intuition. Carla, who came to see me at age 33, is an example.

> "When I walked down the aisle, my stomach felt sick as though my whole body was telling me not to go through with the ceremony. "

I asked Carla why she got married.

> "I did not want to disappoint my parents and my friends. I should have listened to my intuition. My brain kept saying, 'I'll work this out, everything will be ok.' I should have ignored what my mind was saying and listened to my gut."

By the time Carla came to see me, she had two young children, ages seven and nine. Her husband Jim was addicted to church. He attended church meetings several nights a week and volunteered to work on retreats that required him to spend weekends away from home.

I asked Carla if there were other times that she had not followed her gut. As she answered the question, her eyes welled up with tears.

Quote: "The hard thing about denial is you deny you're in it."

- Anonymous

"I've never listened to my intuition. My mother and father are extremely controlling. They're very religious, and I was never free to plan anything for myself. Whenever I had an idea or a strong feeling, they would always have a negative reaction. I learned to listen to them. They made decisions and felt they knew what was best for me."

Tip: In my office, I have a framed graphic image of a Chinese ideogram that means "chaos." Beneath the symbol, it says:

- where brilliant dreams are born

- before the beginning of great brilliance there must be chaos

- before a brilliant person begins something great he/she must look foolish to the crowd

Carla explained that her husband Jim is the son of her father's best friend and that her parents had decided he would be a good match. They liked Jim because he was so devoted to their church.

> "When I told Jim I needed to see a counselor, he wanted me to see the church pastor. We disagreed and he refused to pay for my therapy. My gut told me I not only needed counseling but I also needed financial freedom."

Carla's husband did not want her to work and he became very angry when she told him she wanted to go to nursing school.

> "Some of our biggest fights occurred when I told Jim I wanted to get a part-time job and take classes. He put obstacles in my path at every step and said, over and over, 'women belong in the home.'"

Carla's parents agreed with Jim. They insisted that he was right and told her she did not need an education. They also thought she should see the minister at their church instead of a counselor. In spite of the opposition, Carla started working part time and signed up for classes. When the pressure at home continued for more than a year, she decided to file for a divorce. Her gut told her it was the right decision.

In dysfunctional families, the truth is hidden and family members are in denial.

> "Dad is sick with the flu."

Quote: "Men and women belong to different species and communications between them is still in its infancy."

- Bill Cosby
  Comedian

To say "Dad is sick with the flu" when he is hungover is a classic example of your mind overriding your gut.

Learning to listen to your intuition represents the breaking down of old ideas. In *The Empire Strikes Back*, Luke Skywalker's training subjects him to many tests. Yoda tells him, "You must unlearn what you have learned." The path for the aspiring Jedi is full of trials, and success rests on one's psychological or spiritual condition.

Detective Work: Evaluate What Your Gut Is Telling You

Earlier in the book, I introduced the tool that I use to help my clients get in touch with their feelings. Fear of consequences is often the reason that people do not pay attention to their feelings. If fear is the reason that you're ignoring your gut, assertiveness training may be appropriate. In this section, we'll cover the steps you can use to determine if fear is causing denial, but before we do, here are some important ideas to consider:

Family of Origin

In Chapter 1, we learned about the roles people play in dysfunctional families, including the hero, rebel, clown and lost child. Of these, the rebel will be the one who will be likely to challenge constraints such as cultural traditions. The others will often succumb to social pressure or the expectations of family members regardless of their feelings. Author Amy Tan's *The Joy Luck Club*, adapted for film in 1993, contains many examples of social pressures endured by Asian American women whose mothers experienced hardships when they grew up in China. Each of the mothers are strong but subservient—a characteristic of Chinese women. Actress Rosalind Chao, who plays the part of Rose, is forced to deal with the difficulties of a cultural divide when she falls in love with Andrew McCarthy, who plays Ted, a white classmate who she meets in college. They marry, and although Rose manages to ignore negative reactions from Ted's parents and her mother, Rose's learned subservient behavior drives Ted away. Their marriage looks like it will end in divorce, but Ted is suddenly re-attracted to Rose when she decides to assert herself over the marriage settlement.

Quote: "The most difficult thing is the decision to act; the rest is merely tenacity. The fears are paper tigers. You can do anything you decide to do. You can act to change and control your life; and the procedure, the process is its own reward."

- Amelia Earhart
  Aviator
  First female to fly solo
  from Hawaii to California

Mental Health Is About Choices That Make You Happy

Mental health is about what is right for the individual. It's important to remember that other people are incapable of making the right choices for you. You must make decisions for yourself and follow your gut.

Weighing the Cost of Change

One of the factors that prevents people from making changes is fear of change. What's important to realize is that there are costs associated with change but there are also costs associated with not changing. I call changing the patterns in a relationship, "changing the dance." In *The Joy Luck Club*, Rose changed the dance from a waltz to a slam dance and Ted was turned on. If Rose did not change, her marriage would have ended in divorce, which would have been the cost of not changing. In Rose's case, the amount of change was great. If we were to rate the amount of change on a scale from 1 to 10, Rose's change would be a 10. Given the amount of cultural influence in her life, she had to draw upon a repressed part of her personality and adopt a new role. If you're facing a situation that requires change, ask yourself (on a scale from one to ten):

- How much do I want to change?

- What are the costs related to:

  a.) changing

  b.) not changing

This requires careful consideration of the risks involved, because the cost of not changing may be greater than the cost associated with change.

Quote: "Doubt, indulged and cherished, is in danger of becoming denial; but if honest, and bent on thorough investigation, it may soon lead to full establishment of the truth."

- Ambrose Bierce
  Author and Satirist

Change Takes Practice

Sometimes my clients undershoot or overshoot changes in their behavior and then they need to adjust to find a "center." For example, college-age children from very controlled homes sometimes go crazy when they go away to school. Or, a wife who feels controlled or diminished by her husband blows up and tells her husband off. Occasionally, I hear about the blowup if the husband calls and says, "What did you do?"

Adapting to change can be compared to learning to bounce a basketball. The first time you bounce the ball, it feels clumsy. With practice, you'll be able to bounce the ball with either hand, then dribble and then shoot. Any new experience will feel chaotic at first. Change takes practice and requires that you work through the chaos to arrive at a plateau.

Identify Your Feelings

Earlier, we learned about a scaling tool that's based on four basic feelings: mad, glad, sad and afraid. To determine if it's fear that is keeping you in denial or shielding you from what your gut is telling you, use the scaling tool and pay attention to the score you attach to these feelings. Carla did not do this before she walked down the aisle, but let's suppose she had. How would she scale?

Step 1. Identify a situation that's uncomfortable
The first step requires that you identify a possible uncomfortable situation. In Carla's case, it would have been calling off the wedding.

Quote: "Denial is a common tactic that substitutes deliberate ignorance for thoughtful planning."

- Charles Tremper
  Author, *Risk Management*

Step 2. Attach a score to each feeling

The following example is a template for getting in touch with feelings that you may have trouble accepting or expressing:

Am I feeling Mad? _(yes)_ Intensity?__2___

Am I feeling Glad? _(yes)_ Intensity?__1___

Am I feeling Sad? _(yes)_ Intensity?___2___

Am I feeling Afraid? _(yes)_ Intensity?__5___

Step 3. Try to determine why a score is high

This step requires that you probe and look inward to determine the reason you have assigned a high score to a particular emotion.

In Carla's case, if fear is the reason she did not call off her wedding, it may be that's she was afraid she would

• Be embarrassed

• Disappoint her family

• Disappoint her friends

• Be single

Trusting Your Intuition

Note:

In all the Star Wars films, the Force is the central, mysterious energy that is the key to the magic in the stories. When a Jedi Knight is told to "trust" the Force, he's really being told to trust his intuition. Intuition is a power that eases life's troubles and helps you tune into yourself. When you accept your intuition, doors open, help comes when you need it the most and the impossible becomes possible.

The idea of trusting one's intuition is a new idea for a Jedi Knight just as it is for most people. To accept the concept, one has to abandon ideas that we had previously clung to. In many mystical stories, this is called the "dark night of the soul" because it often requires us to face the unknown without the support of what our mind is telling us. Success rests on one's ability to trust the intuition. Precision is also a must because there is no second-guessing. Luke Skywalker's test is a metaphysical one and his capacity for discernment is within him—just as ours is within us. Our tests are the tools that are used to break down old ideas.

For Carla, trusting her intuition meant she also needed to have the courage to stand up to her husband and parents, who were making her decisions. Just as learning to walk or swim takes time, so does learning to listen to your intuition. When Carla became aware of her intuition, it represented an important phase of her personal growth. She simultaneously stood up to her family and unblocked a bridge between her inner and outer consciousness. Today, she has a very good job as a nurse and she has learned to listen to her intuition.

Quote: "From the moment I picked your book up until I laid it down, I was convulsed with laughter. Someday I intend reading it."

- Groucho Marx
American Comedian

"I thought the feeling I had in my gut was from the food at the rehearsal dinner. I guess there was more to it."

Notes

Chapter 11

RULE #11

Denial is Necessary and Normal, But Too Much Denial Makes You Stupid

If there are angry or irritated people all around you, it's a clue that you're in denial.

"Denial is a large part of what keeps people stuck in old patterns and behaviors. Ironically, denial also keeps us from being hospitalized with major anxiety disorders. If we allowed ourselves to project into the future and try to figure out all the bad things that would/could happen, we could not survive. As a result, denial keeps anxiety in check but it has the potential to shield us from what can make us grow."

An Elephant in the Middle of the Room

Note:
Denial is often the result of a child believing he/she is bad. This same child also idealizes the family or parents.

Later in this chapter, I describe the difference between benign denial and toxic denial. When someone is in toxic denial, whatever it is that they are ignoring may be considered to be an "elephant in the middle of the room." At first, they walk around the edge of the room and pretend the elephant is not there. By looking only at the walls, they never have to actually *look* at the elephant. They stay entirely in the perimeter of the room, refusing to even acknowledge that the room has an elephant in the center. They could see the elephant if they looked—but they're not going to.

Letting Go of Denial

Letting go of denial requires steps that include:

Acknowledging the elephant (letting go)
This is the first step toward letting go of denial.

Stop caring about the elephant (detachment)
Detachment is the necessary next step because trying to make the elephant go away causes problems.

Taking the focus off the elephant (refocusing)
By taking your focus off the elephant, the elephant gets smaller. A healthy focus involves balance.

Prevent the Elephant from Dominating Your Life

The truth is, the elephant will never go away. However, the key is to prevent the elephant from dominating your life and to avoid getting trampled. A very small elephant will never be able to damage one's life. By focusing on

Quote: "A journey is like marriage. The certain way to be wrong is to think you control it."

- John Steinbeck
Author
The Grapes of Wrath
The Pearl
Of Mice and Men

one's own life instead of on the elephant, the elephant will shrink into a corner of the room where it can't possibly be the center of attention.

"Thanks for showing me the house. It was hard to see the living room with that elephant in the way."

Meet Carol

Note:
*Author John Bradshaw, who
has written several books about
families, explains that people
from dysfunctional households
are fantasy-bound to their family.
They frequently defend parents
against any suggestion that they
did less than a sterling job. They
also continually try to please
their parents to win their love.*

Denial is choosing to look away from events in our lives that we don't want to deal with. It's one of several psychological defenses that people use to deal with stress or trauma. It's also an important mechanism that gives us time to come to terms with reality. In moderation, denial is a valuable tool that can help us manage our emotions. However, a massive amount of denial can also lead to problems. A 2002 television drama that is based on true events illustrates the consequences of avoiding what is accessible to our conscious minds if we really look.

In March of 2002, Court TV aired "Guilt By Association," in which actress Mercedes Ruehl played the part of Susan Walker. Susan is a hardworking widow and mother of two young children whose new boyfriend is arrested on drug charges. She's arrested as a coconspirator even though she knows nothing about her boyfriend's drug sales. Although she is set up, she's found guilty and sentenced to 20 years. Susan could not help the prosecutors build a case against the people involved. Sadly, she knew no actual facts about their involvement but she did recall having a feeling that something was not quite right.

Although the TV drama was filmed to draw attention to unjust mandatory minimum sentencing laws, it could be said that women who date drug dealers have a heavy case of denial. There are usually clues that they choose to ignore. This is true in many different types of situations. Carol, who came to see me at age 30, is an example of a woman who ignored clues about an abuser. When she met him, there were details about his behavior that might have saved her a great deal of trauma.

Quote: "You take the blue pill and you wake up in your bed and believe whatever you want to believe. You take the red pill, and you stay in wonderland and see how deep the rabbit hole goes."

- Morpheus
The Matrix

"When I met Ben, he had a beautiful car and nice clothes, and he was very polite. At the bar where we met, I did notice that everyone seemed to steer clear of him. He'd talk about people who betrayed him but never explained why. That should have set off my alarm but it didn't."

When I asked Carol to describe Ben's negative behavior in more detail, she said:

"Ben showered me with attention at first. He sent flowers, he opened doors and he started calling me every night. The trouble occurred when he asked me who I spent time with. He acted as though he did not want me to see my friends."

At this point in the relationship, Carol's internal set of red flags should have alerted her that Ben would want to control every aspect of her life. Unfortunately, Carol was in denial. Her mind told her that Ben loved her and that he wanted to be with her at all times. Her mind also told her that he wanted to protect her. She listened to what her mind told her instead of her gut.

"I felt so isolated in my relationship with Ben. He tried to cut off my relationships with my friends. In spite of our problems, I thought if I was nurturing enough, things would calm down and he'd be more reasonable. I was mistaken."

Quote: I want to believe.

- Fox Mulder's poster
The X-Files

The dues Carol had to pay for her denial turned out to be severe. Ben beat her and she ended up in the hospital. Physical pain and the threat of dying made Carol start counseling. When Carol went to the police to get a restraining order, she discovered he already had a police record. Ben had severely beaten three other women. The probation officer helped Carol get rid of Ben by threatening prison.

Meet Stephanie

Note:
People who are in denial often minimize their parents' physical punishments. The idea that they can control physical abuse by being perfect is left over from their childhood.

When denial becomes paralyzing, the people around you often become frustrated or angry at your behavior. They can see the elephant even if you can't. Stephanie, a mother of three girls, is an example. She came to see me due to a mandate by social services. Her fourteen-year-old daughter had accused her mother's boyfriend of sexual molestation and Stephanie felt her daughter was lying.

> "Social services took my daughter away from me. She told a friend of hers that my boyfriend molested her and her friend told her counselor. My daughter is furious with me because I don't believe her. My sister is also furious with me because I've defended my boyfriend. I don't think he has molested my daughter."

Stephanie's own father molested her from age five to ten. Although her boyfriend claims he did not molest Stephanie's fourteen-year-old daughter, he has a history of sexual abuse. He was previously brought up on charges for molesting the child of a previous girlfriend and was acquitted because there was not enough evidence. Stephanie's own psychological pain concerning the abuse in her own childhood is what is causing her denial. As a result, she is unable to admit that her boyfriend may be guilty.

Sometimes, a massive amount of denial can exist in families even though many of the members know the truth. Those who know the truth are often angry or hurt. The anger surrounding the denial is often one of the best clues that denial exists. Stephanie's daughter and sister were both furious with her.

Benign Denial vs. Toxic Denial

Note:
A person who is in denial believes that everything is OK in spite of facts that say the opposite.

If you've ever seen a speedo bikini on someone without a waist, you've seen a person who is in denial. Then there's the teenager who's read the *Cliff Notes* version of Dicken's *Great Expectations* without reading the book and feels he's ready for his exam. Believing that you have an athlete's body when you don't or believing that you're ready for an exam when you've read a 100-page booklet instead of the 544-page classic is benign denial. It's foolish but it's harmless. Other examples include:

- A teen who forms a band and believes he'll be a famous rock star.

- An aging actress who works as a waitress and continues to ask her photographer friend to update her 8 X 10 headshots years after she has had her last audition for a paying part.

- A bald man who believes his synthetic toupee looks like real hair.

- People who buy wrinkle removing or cellulite vanishing creams.

Toxic denial is much more serious, and it involves a threat to someone's well-being—either your own or someone you're involved with. Examples include a person who has not confronted his/her addiction to a harmful substance or someone who has not owned up to the fact that he or she is in a relationship with a spendaholic or a gambler.

Identifying Denial

Denial is a distortion of reality that causes us to rationalize a problem to minimize pain. It forms a cushion that shields us from the facts. Realizing that you or someone you love is in denial is often a painful experience, but it can lead to personal growth. The first step includes identifying denial.

Clues About the Stages of Denial

Here are some clues about the stages of denial:

Does Not Know the Problem Exists
There's an Arab proverb that describes four kinds of people. It says that three of the types are to be avoided and the fourth cultivated (*Note: the comments in italics are mine*): those who don't know that they don't know (*totally oblivious*); those who know that they don't know (*too lazy to do their homework*); those who don't know that they know (*denying their gut*) and those who know that they know (*paying attention to their gut*).

Does Not Believe There Is a Problem
A person's belief systems will have a powerful effect on his/her experiences or what they perceive as reality. These people know that a situation exists but they do not believe it is a problem. Families often teach people not to trust their gut. A classic example is "Dad has the flu" instead of "Dad has a hangover." Dysfunctional families have very powerful rules and boundaries that prohibit full expression of feelings, needs and wants. Addiction is just one example of dysfunction. Other examples include an emotionally distant or absent parent or some trauma that involves physical or emotional abuse. In these circumstances,

Quote: "I'm not in denial, I'm just selective about the reality I choose to accept."

- *Calvin and Hobbes*
  Comic Strip
  by Bill Watterson

denial becomes unconscious over time and grief is usually left unresolved.

Believes He/She Can Control the Problem

There's a self-confidence that often accompanies belief systems, and that self-confidence can cause a person to believe that he/she is in control of a problem.

Denial Creates Adults With Unresolved Emotions

An adult child is a person who looks and acts like an adult but has unresolved childhood emotions from growing up in a dysfunctional family that is steeped in denial. These emotions are often destuctive, and can show up in many different forms of self-destructive behavior.

Denial Can Lead to Feelings of Abandonment

The strict rules and boundaries in dysfunctional families that enable family members to avoid dealing with trauma and unresolved issues can make a person feel abandoned. Abandonment stimulates grief, and grief that is not resolved leads to blocked feelings that are either acted out in similar experiences or in compulsive behavior.

Quote: "Success or failure depends more upon attitude than upon capacity. Successful men act as though they have accomplished or are enjoying something. Soon it becomes a reality. Act, look, feel successful, conduct yourself accordingly, and you will be amazed at the positive results."

- William James
  American Philosopher

Feelings About Trauma Can Lead to Unresolved Grief

There is a strong relationship between denial and grief in dysfunctional families. When children experience the trauma of abuse, there is usually an enormous amount of hurt and pain that needs to be validated and discharged. When families avoid traumatizing events, the issues are usually reenacted in the next generation.

Does Not Notice Other People's Reactions to a Problem

When someone is in toxic denial, it's very likely that the people around him/her are not in denial. It's also likely that they are frustrated or even angry. Reactions of friends and relatives often help when you're trying to identify denial.

Asleep In Our Original Trance

Identifying denial is a process that does not happen overnight. The work involved is often related to our family of origin. Author John Bradshaw refers to denial as mystification. He says, "We are to some degree still mystified—still asleep in our original trances playing out the role in our family system needed to maintain balance and control."

Meet Dennis

Note:
In a codependent family system, problems and bad behavior are usually reinforced.

At times, family members who know the truth are angry for different reasons. Denial also may exist in different forms within a family. Dennis' family is an example. His wife Claire had a cocaine habit that caused her to manipulate him financially. He, in turn, manipulated his parents into giving him large sums of money that they kept a secret from the rest of the family. Over time, clues about Claire's habit became apparent, and a complex problem took shape involving several family members who were all in denial.

During the ten years that Dennis received $350,000, his brother and two sisters were kept in the dark about the total transfer of money. Although they did not have all the facts, it could be said that they were in partial denial because they never questioned any of the clues in plain sight. In part, this was due to the fact that they had a parent who was stingy with money. He had trained them never to ask for anything. This childhood conditioning carried over into their adult life and prevented them from asking questions. Here are some details about Dennis and his family:

Family Member	Denial
Dennis	Dennis is in denial about the fact that his wife is a cocaine user. He knows she's not spending large sums on clothes or other material possessions but never questions her about her spending.

Family Member	Denial
Ed (Dennis' Father)	Ed is also in denial about how large sums of money are being used. Without asking for a truthful explanation, he's been giving money to his son for ten years
Virginia (Dennis' Mother)	Virginia knows her husband is stingy with his other children yet watches him give Dennis $350,000 over the course of ten years. After years of marriage to someone who has strict control of their finances, Virginia feels that she has no power when it comes to making decisions about money. Like her husband, she remains in the dark about how the money is being used and convinces herself that the help they're providing their son is justified. Neither she nor her husband think about how their other children might feel if they knew about the $350,000 including her daughter, whose husband has been out of work for over two years.
Walter (Dennis' brother)	Walter knows that Dennis makes $80-90,000 as an accountant. Although he does not know about the transfer of money, he notes that his parents have given Dennis substantial gifts over a ten-year period. Instead of making any inquiries, he thinks about the fact that his stingy father is finally showing signs of generosity—and considers this a good thing.
Susan (Dennis' sister)	Susan was the first to know about the ten-year transfer of money but kept the news from her brother and sister. Her mother Virginia had asked her not to tell anyone and she kept her promise for a year. Like her siblings, Susan is conditioned not to ask questions related to money.

Family Member	Denial
Julie (Dennis' other sister)	Julie's husband has health problems and has been out of work for over two years. When she learns about the money that her parents gave to her brother, she is very stunned but remains silent.

Clues No One Wanted to Acknowledge

While Dennis' father was in the hospital, he asked his daughter Susan to help him with his bookkeeping, a project that led to the discovery of Ed and Dennis' ten-year secret. When they had a chance to air their feelings, they realized they all felt hurt. Today, when they talk over the details of the ten-year money transfer, they all realize that there were clues that they refused to acknowledge:

Cars as Gifts
Over a ten-year period, Dennis received four cars from Ed and Virginia, who are otherwise very stingy. Although the spouses of the siblings were bothered that they were never offered any of the cars, Dennis' brother and sisters seemed to accept the idea.

Home Improvements
Dennis purchased a home in a high-end neighborhood and added expensive improvements such as an underground sprinkling system.

Trips to Florida
Ed and Virginia spent their winters in Florida. Even though Dennis always claimed to be financially strapped, he took his family to Florida every year to visit his parents. Again, Walter's, Susan's and Julie's spouses won-

Quote: "Fear leads to anger, anger leads to hate, and hate leads to suffering."

- Yoda
  Star Wars

dered if Ed and Virginia paid for Dennis' trips but everyone remained silent. No one wanted to consider that Ed and Virginia had acted with favoritism.

Ed Had Trained His Family Not to Talk About Money

As time went on, it was Julie's financial situation that nudged her brother and sister out of their denial. Her husband was unemployed and her family was living on her teacher's aide salary of $10 an hour. Susan spoke up and asked her parents to help Julie instead of Dennis and she broke the news of the $350,000 to Julie and Walter.

Because her father had always made it clear that he resented any request for financial help, all three of Dennis' siblings had learned not to ask their parents for anything. If Julie's financial situation had not turned dire, they may never have talked about finances. When they did begin to talk about money and compare notes, they all learned the truth about their father's stingy attitude. Because no one had ever talked about money, they learned that there were many family secrets. Julie and Susan had both paid for their own weddings, while Walter paid for his college education, and these facts were hidden until they compared stories.

Susan, who is nine years younger than Walter, remembered what a struggle Walter had when he had to ask his parents for a $50 per month allowance throughout his college years. The argument about the $50 was something she had accidentally heard and that he chose to forget. Walter, Julie and Susan knew that Ed had paid for Dennis' education and a lavish wedding and they were baffled by the inconsistency.

What was particularly hurtful was the fact that Ed's fortune was inheritance he had received from his father. Ed's father had left him more than half a million dollars that he had used to set up a life estate for both Ed and his children. Now it appeared that a large portion of the life estate had been siphoned off in payments to Dennis.

Did Ed, Virginia, Dennis and Claire Change?

Even though Ed knew about Julie's financial struggle, he never offered to help her. Julie had learned *not* to ask her parents for help and had been disappointed when she turned to them for help in the past. It was through her sister Susan's appeals that they began to give Julie a minimal amount of help. Susan's intervention eventually led to group sessions with all of the siblings. When they met to talk over the truth, Dennis said he felt bad that there had been an unequal amount of gifts and he also realized that he and his wife needed therapy. He agreed to take his wife to counseling and explore Al-Anon, a group that helps families of those who are struggling with an addiction. Ed and Virginia refused to join therapy sessions or make amends by equaling out the gift-giving. They did realize that their money gifts to Dennis exacerbated his problem and they agreed to stop. Unfortunately, Ed would not acknowledge how their extreme favoritism hurt their other three children. His wife Virginia admits that the gifts to Dennis were unfair and she's trying to encourage Ed to fix things even though he refuses to admit he made a mistake. Her actions exhibit a codependent dynamic. She could act independently and fix the unequal distribution of money with money from her own trust, but she will not go against her husband.

Breaking Through Toxic Denial

If denial is a refusal to admit the truth, then a breakthrough occurs when the party in denial sees the truth about a person or a situation.

Circumstances That Help Break Through Denial

The circumstances that bring this about can be external or internal. Examples include:

Crisis (External)

A crisis brought about by the buildup of a threat to well-being can lead to a breakthrough. However, it can also push a person further into denial. If the person retreats deeper into denial, there may be a serious addiction problem or a personalilty disorder, a subject we will cover in the last chapter.

Self-Discovery (Internal)

Truth that is unearthed through the process of self-discovery usually occurs when the party in denial does his/her homework. As FBI man Fox Mulder from the *The X-Files* says, "The truth is out there." If the denial involves a situation, self-discovery can be accomplished through research at the library or on the Internet. If the denial involves another person's behavior, self-discovery can be accomplished through counseling, a 12-Step program, or through long talks with supportive friends.

Scenarios That Illustrate How Denial Works

When people face their denial, it's usually after a buildup that leads them to discover what is happening. In order for the reader to understand that a person in denial may either have a breakthrough or go deeper into denial, I have organized this section with probability tracks:

Situation	Build-up to a Crisis
Tom has been losing weight and throwing up for a year. He's been reporting his symptoms to a doctor who gives him medication for an ulcer.	Tom's weight loss accelerates, he completely loses his appetite and throws up blood. Even though his mother, wife and sister are pushing him to see a doctor, he ignores them.
Susan's husband has a drug addiction that he is hiding from her. Although they're frequently strapped for money, he's away a lot and tells her that he's working. She feels uncomfortable with his stories but believes him.	Susan receives notices from their bank and finds out that her husband has not paid the mortgage in two months. Her husband recently passed out at work and was taken to a local emergency room where he was given a drug screening. When the screening came back positive for Vicodan and marijuana, he was told that he must go to drug treatment or be fired.
Jim owns and manages a hardware store that has been a source of income to his family for three generations. When Home Depot built a chain store in a new mall outside his town, his own store's revenue dropped 35% and business continues to decline.	The hardware store does not have enough cash to pay all of the employees.

Probability Track #1 (Breakthrough)	Probability Track #2 (Deeper in Denial)
Tom goes to a different doctor and learns that he is seriously ill with cancer but finally pursues proper treatment.	Tom stays with the same doctor and continues to take ulcer medication.
Susan's husband goes to drug treatment, learns about his addiction, and works toward becoming drug-free.	Susan's husband blames his employer for taking him to the emergency room where he was given a drug screening. He goes to the union and tries to have his drug screening thrown out. He does not want to go to drug treatment and wants to have any mention of drug treatment removed from his record.
Jim asks the store's accountant to do an audit and look at his partner's recent spending patterns. He hires a private detective to determine if his partner is embezzling money.	Jim refuses to watch the store's revenue drop and blames the economy. He refinances his house to raise the cash that's needed to keep his business open and to pay his employees.

Notes

Chapter 12

RULE #12

The Best Predictor of Future Behavior Is Past Behavior Unless the Person Works Very Hard to Change

It's very hard to alter behavior.

"One of the hardest lessons I've learned as a therapist concerns negative entrenched behavior patterns. Destructive behavior is not only hard on the person with the problem, but it's also hard on everyone around them.

Even if a person wants to change, it's still very hard. However, if someone works hard enough they can change, and it's amazing to watch. I have always felt honored to be part of the process."

Predictive Behavior

Remember the story of Peter Pan? At twelve, he hears his mother talking about school and marriage and he runs away. Tinkerbell, a tiny fairy, rescues him. She takes him to a land where he'll never have to be a man. In Neverland, Peter can stay dirty, taunt pirates, never feel and never fall in love. Peter sings:

> "I don't want to grow up. I don't want to grow up."

Peter never changes—not even for Wendy, a young girl whom he takes with him to Neverland. Wendy, who loves Peter, finally leaves him because she knows he will never change.

A Person's History

Behavior is predictive, and a person's history will help you determine how serious they are about change. Clues to watch for:

- Is the person determined?

- How pervasive is their negative behavior?

- Does the person have a support system for their negative behavior?

- Does the person have a support system for their positive behavior?

- What is the cost of changing?

- What is the cost of not changing?

- Are there any rewards for changing?

- Are there any rewards for not changing?

FYI: Therapists often talk amongst themselves about the difficulties involved in the diagnosis of personality disorders. Getting acquainted with their traits is useful for everyone ("forewarned is forearmed"). Because the traits are pervasive, it's useful to ask questions about a person's relationships with other people. Dr. Paul Frechette, a former psychiatrist at Crossroads, used to have an expression. He'd say, "History, history, history...."

Making an Assessment

Later in this chapter, we'll present a questionnaire that is designed to help you determine how likely it is that someone will change. If the answer to all of the questions on the questionnaire is "no," it's unlikely that the person will change. If you are in denial and have dreams and fantasies about someone in your life, then your goal will be to break through your denial.

You'll also read about June, my patient who had unrealistic ideas about changes she wanted to see in her mother's behavior. June wanted an unconditionally nurturing mother, and unfortunately her wish could not be fulfilled. Her mother was incapable of change.

When you break through denial, you'll always adapt in a positive way. You may not need to end the relationship. The key to your mental health is to break through denial. When this occurs, you will be able to make adjustments that are more rewarding. If the person is a toxic parent, you will be able to understand the need for creating boundaries or limits.

Meet June

June, age 25, came to see me about her controlling mother. Her father left when June was three years old. Just out of college, June would like to move out of her mother's house, but her mother wants her to stay and save money.

> "My mother is very involved in my life. She buys my clothes, she makes appointments for me to get a haircut and she makes every decision about the food we get for the meals we prepare. I'm not allowed to have any choices. She's also critical of the men whom I date and she's broken up a few of my relationships. She has no friends of her own. I feel trapped."

I asked June if her mother has ever tried to change.

> "When I confronted my mother about her control, she promised to change. She said if I live with her for another six months, she'll give me a lot more freedom."

Next, I asked June if there was any evidence in her mother's history that would convince her that she would live up to her promise.

> "Not really. We have had several fights and she says I will see a lot of changes. I'm afraid if I move out, my mother will kill herself."

One important question remained. Did her mother ever try to kill herself in the past?

Tip: *Who Moved My Cheese? An Amazing Way to Deal with Change in Your Work and in Your Life* by Spencer Johnson teaches us that change can be a blessing or a curse, depending on your perspective.

"My mother has always threatened to kill herself but she's never actually attempted suicide."

After several months, June moved out of her mother's house, but her struggle was not over. At one point, June came to a session with tears in her eyes.

"I don't know how to deal with my mother. She calls me ten times a day and she's constantly threatening to kill herself. I feel very guilty."

June continued to feel guilty and I asked her why she felt guilt.

"The Bible says, 'Honor Thy Mother' doesn't it? She's all I have and I'm all she has."

June and I talked about guilt at many of her sessions. Feelings of guilt are only good for the short run. Guilt is a negative emotion. A person who feels guilty needs to examine whether they have truly done something wrong. If so, that person needs to make amends. If not, then the guilt should be considered to be toxic shame that needs to be examined and given up.

I asked her about her other feelings.

"I feel happy and free. I also feel tremendous independence, and that feels wonderful. I'm finally able to go out and do things."

Quote: We all have big changes in our lives that are more or
less a second chance.

- Harrison Ford
   Actor

Next, I asked her if she thought she is supposed to give up her life for her mother.

"I used to feel that way but I'm starting to question it."

When June admitted that she thought about giving up her life for her mother, I asked, "If you had a child, would you want a similar relationship with your child?"

"No! I would want my child to feel free and happy."

Next, I asked, "Would you want your best friend to have a similar relationship?"

"No! I would want my friend to feel free."

I told June to treat herself as her best friend.

"It's hard. I know I need to keep setting bound-aries and limits for my mother. I know that I need to be independent. My biggest fear is that my mother will never change and that I will need to give up my relationship with her. I'm afraid we will never be able to be close again."

I told June that she needed to accept the truth of her mother's capacity to change. There is a chance that her mother's emotional pain will prompt her to seek help. At this point, it's still uncertain whether her mother would

Quote: "You must be the change you wish to see in the world."

- Gandhi

eventually change. I told June that she's raised her mother long enough and that it's time for her mother to live on her own.

The dance of June's relationship with her mother ebbed and flowed. In a relationship dance, if one person stops, the other person cannot dance. However, this does not mean that a partner's negative behavior will stop. In fact, it will probably escalate in an attempt to intimidate the healthier partner into continuing the dance. When June stopped, her mother's behavior escalated and she used all of her controlling strategies to try to restore her relationship with June.

In the next section, we'll take a look at behavior modification techniques that June would need to adopt.

Behavior Modification

To stop her mother's negative behavior, June needed to apply behavior modification techniques. By understanding the principles involved, she increased the likelihood of success. The concepts that are important to behavior modification include:

Clarity
June needed to be very clear when she described the behavior she found unacceptable.

Consistency
Once June established new boundaries, she needed to be consistent and not revert to previous behavior patterns.

Patience
In order for behavior modification to work, June will need to be patient. In the process, she'll discover what behavioral scientists call extinction bursts and spikes that will test her resolve.

> **Extinction Burst** – an increase in bad behavior. During this time, June's mother will most likely increase the number of threats and display behavior that is much worse (See Figure). This is often the hardest time to be consistent and patient.

> **Decrease in Behavior** – If June does not give in to her mother's threats, she will see a decrease in her bad behavior (See Figure).

> **Behavior Spike** – Change never occurs overnight. With time, June is bound to notice behavior spikes. However, if she continues to be patient and consistent,

Quote: "If you don't like something, change it. If you can't change it, change your attitude. Don't complain."

— Maya Angelou
Poet

her mother's negative behavior will decrease. Ideally, her mother will realize that if she wants a relationship with June, she will need to exhibit positive behavior (See Figure).

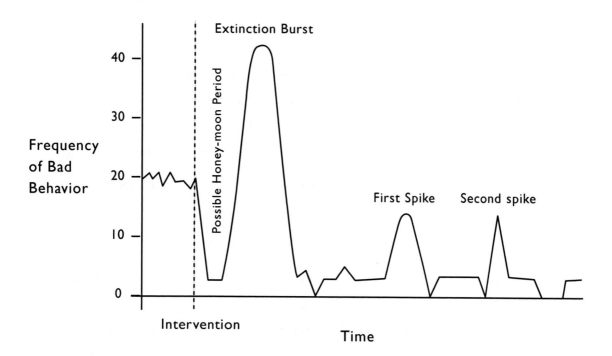

Your Detective Work

When a client is uncertain if someone in their life will change, we look critically at whether the person's traits are persistent. If you are in a situation that is similar to June's, here are some important questions to ask:

1. How pervasive is the person's behavior?

    a. Has he/she always been this way?

    b. Does he/she behave this way with other people?

    c. Does your family behave this way?

    d. Does he/she say they will change and then revert back to their previous behavior?

2. How insightful are they? In other words, do they think about how they think?

3. Does he/she admit that they're wrong?

4. Does he/she admit that they have a problem?

5. Does he/she blame other people?

6. Is he/she judgmental?

7. Does he/she show a curiosity about life or other people?

8. Is he/she accepting of others' ways of being?

9. Would you describe this person as stubborn?

10. Is he/she working hard on changing their behavior?

11. Is he/she talking about change?

12. Is he/she willing to seek therapy?

Chapter 13

RULE #13

Don't Take It Personally, It's Just Their Personality (Disorder) —They Do This to Everyone

"Insane people are always sure they are fine. It's only the sane people who are willing to admit they are crazy."

Nora Ephron

"Evil is the exercise of power, the imposing of one's will upon others by overt or covert coercion."

Scott Peck,
People of the Lie

"One of the hardest things for therapists to learn is that there are people who have a different type of conscience— if any. Therapists consistently underestimate people with personality disorders and they have a hard time with diagnosis and treatment. At Crossroads, we developed a psychological screening test to identify personality disorders because they have a tendency to fool you. Many people who come to Crossroads for counseling are the codependent victims of people who have personality disorders, and it's typical for these people to endure untold pain and suffering. They're handcuffed by naivete and false hopes that their loved one will change when there is little or no chance that this will happen. This chapter is devoted to them."

Learning About Personality Disorders

Many years ago, I counseled a woman who was married to a man with a personality disorder, and a statement she made about her husband provides a perfect description of his problem:

> "We stayed up last night and spoke for four hours and I felt he understood me. Then he woke up and he was exactly the same as he was before our talk. If he were a computer, he behaved as though he had erased his entire hard drive."

Most people who have a deep personal conversation for four hours will take it to heart and not "erase their hard drive." This is one of the most important points to learn in this chapter. Here are all the important points:

- People with destructive personality disorders are not like you and me. They are predators who are incapable of empathy (*Note: Not all personality disorders are destructive. The disorders that negatively effect relationships are described in the pages that follow*).

- Their behavior is pervasive, which means that they end up treating everyone the same (*Note: Destructive traits may not be apparent when you first get to know someone with a personality disorder*).

- If you are in a relationship with a person who has a personality disorder, you need to understand that they will probably never substantially change. They will not fill your unmet needs.

Quote: "The normal person is likely to consume a moderate amount of social approval—verbal and non-verbal—in the form of affirmation, attention, or admiration. The narcissist is the mental equivalent of an alcoholic. He asks for more and yet more. He directs his whole behavior, in fact his life, to obtain these pleasurable tidbits of human attention."

- Dr. Sam Vaknin
Malignant Self Love

In the United States, it is estimated that personality disorders (PDs) affect 10-15 percent of the population. The *Merck Manual of Diagnosis and Therapy*[1] provides a definition:

> "Pervasive, inflexible and stable personality traits that deviate from cultural norms and cause distress or functional impairment."

Destructive Personality Disorders

Although there are many different types of personality disorders, we will cover the three that are the most damaging to personal relationships:

- Narcissist
- Antisocial or Sociopath
- Borderline Personality Disorder

Although people with personality disorders mellow later in life, in their youth they are very rigid. In this chapter, we will focus on how to identify and avoid them.

Personality Disorder Traits

It's important to understand that the percentage of the population with a pure personality disorder is very small. It is much more common to see people with personality disorder traits, and we use the word "traited" to refer to this group. The traited group can be helped. Although it is hard for them to feel empathy for other people, they can be trained.

[1] Merck & Co., Inc. is a pharmaceutical company that has been publishing medical information manuals since 1899.

Quote: "The source of all the narcissist's problems is the belief that human relationships invariably end in humiliation, betrayal, pain and abandonment. This conviction is the outcome of indoctrination in early childhood by their parents, peers, or role models."

- Dr. Sam Vaknin
Malignant Self Love

Personality Disorder Clusters

Although it is beyond the scope of this book, it's also important to mention personality disorder clusters. The American Psychiatric Association's *Diagnostic and Statistical Manual of Mental Disorders (DSM)* is a widely used manual used for diagnosing mental disorders. Each year, the *DSM* is refined and expanded to include new developments in mental health. The *DSM-III* appeared in 1980 and was introduced as a classification system based on a majority opinion of people who represent American mental health specialists. The *DSM-IV* was published in 1994 and the *DSM-V* will not appear until 2010 or later. The *DSM* uses the term "comorbidity" to refer to people who are diagnosed with more than one personality disorder. The traits of those suffering from a personality disorder often follow a pattern. As a result, the American Psychiatric Association has created the following comorbidity "clusters":

- Cluster A
  A cluster A personality may include paranoid personality disorder, schizoid personality disorder and schizotypal personality disorder.

- Cluster B
  A cluster B personality may include narcissistic personality disorder, borderline personality disorder, antisocial personality disorder and histrionic personality disorder (Note: I consider the histrionic personality to be a benign narcissist).

It's important to note that mental health classification is not an exact science. One of the reasons that clinicians use clusters as definitions is because the characteristics of the destructive personality disorders are very similar. Again, the

Quote: "The narcissist hates adults and is repelled by them. In his mind, he is forever innocent and loveable. Being a child, he feels no need to acquire adult skills or adult qualifications. Many a narcissist do not complete their academic studies, refuse to marry or have children, or even get a driver's license. They feel that people should adore them as they are and supply them with all the needs that they, as children, cannot themselves secure."

- Dr. Sam Vaknin
Malignant Self Love

most important goal in this chapter is not to learn about all of the separate personality characteristics but to understand that the person with a personality disorder is not like you and me, their behavior is pervasive, they're incapable of meeting another person's needs, and they're not going to change.

"I don't care if it's a boy or girl as long as I get my figure back."

A Codependent's Guide to Personality Disorders

Note:
The only people who will tolerate people with destructive personality disorders for any length of time are people with low self-esteem.

If you're in a relationship with a personality disordered person, there's a high probability that you are a codependent. This section is designed to illustrate the traits of the Cluster B personality disorders. If you recognize the traits of someone you know, I've provided some strategies for coping with these people later in this chapter.

Profile	Clues	How Pervasive?
Steve, age 22, just got in trouble again for *selling marijuana* to an undercover cop. Although his parents have tried hard to set limits, they're convinced that he *doesn't have a conscience.* He has *stolen things all his life.* When he was eight, he was picked up for shoplifting $50 worth of CDs. He's been on *juvenile probation* for years and went to school *only when he wanted to.* He *does just as he pleases*, and lies constantly. He was kicked out of his grade school for biting and had to leave high school because of an assault and battery charge.	Steve has an antisocial personality disorder. The clues include: • he consistently lies • he's had violent behavior since grade school • he has stolen things all his life • he was kicked out of grade school and high school *Note*: A nomal kid can get into a fight and even get kicked out of school once.	There's evidence that Steve's behavior is very pervasive.

Profile	Clues	How Pervasive?
Wade, a 23-year-old college grad, has a new girlfriend named Jackie who he met at a bar. At first, Jackie liked all the things that Wade liked and *treated him like a god*—just a couple days after she was *released from an in-patient treatment center for bulimia.* Wade says their relationship was like heaven for about two months and then it *shifted and became hell.* When he went out of town for work, *she couldn't go with him and reacted by calling him horrible names, accused him of things he didn't do,* and *threatened him with bodily harm. She also slit her wrists in front of Wade and had to be taken to the hospital.* She's always angry at most of her friends and family members. When Wade talked to two of Jackie's ex-boyfriends, they said she was crazy.	Jackie is a borderline personality disorder. The clues include: • she has few long-term relationships • she's angry at her friends and family members • She treated Wade like a god—and then this shifted and became hell • suicide attempts	Jackie's behavior seems to be very pervasive.

Narcissist (or Narcissist Traits)

Note:
Narcissists demand uninterrupted empathy, and when you stop, they get angry and blame you forever.

The word narcissist is derived from a Greek legend about a mythological character named Narcissus. Having rejected the advances of many girls, Narcissus is punished by Nemesis, the Greek goddess of divine justice. After hearing many rejected girls' prayers for vengeance, Nemesis arranges for Narcissus to fall in love with his own reflection. Obsession with the self and an all-pervasive need for admiration to the exclusion of all others is a key trait in the narcissistic personality.

The Talented Mr. Ripley: A Movie About Narcissism

In other chapters, we've explored movies and characters that have helped us to understand human nature. *The Talented Mr. Ripley*, a story about three Americans living in Italy in the 1950s, is about narcissism. The film's two male leads are both spine-chilling narcissists and against a backdrop of Italy's historical architecture is a story about ethics. Tom Ripley (Matt Damon) is a struggling New York piano tuner, who, due to timing and a case of mistaken identity, is offered $1,000 to go to Europe and persuade the son of a shipping magnate to return home.

Dickey Greenleaf (Jude Law) is the rich son who's adopted a hedonistic lifestyle in Italy. When he's not spending time with his fiancée Marge (Gwyneth Paltrow), Dickey is sailing, drinking and carousing. From the start, the director shows us that Ripley is seduced by Dickey's lush life. As a narcissist, Ripley is driven by jealousy of what Dickey has—power, money and success. Ripley will go to any length to emulate Dickey and his plan gradually turns into a full-blown masquerade. The movie turns dark when Ripley decides to take over Dickey's life and Dickey mysteriously disappears.

Quote: "Love is patient, love is kind. It does not envy, it does not boast, it is not proud. It is not rude, it is not self-seeking, it is not easily angered, it keeps no records of wrong. Love does not delight in evil but rejoices with the truth. It always protects, always trusts, always hopes, always perseveres."

1 Corinthians
13:4-7

In his treatment of women, we see that Dickey is also a narcissist. Besides Marge, he also has an Italian girlfriend who gets into trouble and is turned down when she asks Dickey for help. We see Dickey's cold-hearted narcissistic nature when he says, "I can not help you, go away, you bore me." The film is a Hitchcockian thriller that teaches us the truth about narcissists—they have no feeling for others. They manipulate everyone and only use people.

Personality Criteria

Narcissists have a pervasive pattern of grandiosity (fantasy or behavior), a need for attention and they lack empathy. This behavior begins by early adulthood and it is present in a variety of contexts, as indicated by five (or more) of the following (from *The Diagnostic and Statistical Manual of Mental Disorders)*:

- Grandiose sense of self-importance (e.g., exaggerates achievements and talents, expects to be recognized as superior without commensurate achievements)

- Preoccupied with fantasies of unlimited success, power, brilliance, beauty or ideal love

- Believes that he or she is "special" and unique and can only be understood by, or should associate with, other special or high-status people (or institutions)

- Requires excessive admiration

- Has a sense of entitlement, i.e., unreasonable expectations of especially favorable treatment or automatic compliance with his or her expectations

Quote: "Well-ordered self-love is right and natural."

- Saint Thomas Aquinas

- Is interpersonally exploitative, i.e., takes advantage of others to achieve his or her own ends

- Lacks empathy: is unwilling to recognize or identify with the feelings and needs of others

- Often envious of others or believes that others are envious of him or her

- Shows arrogant, haughty behaviors or attitudes

Antisocial (or Antisocial Traits)

Note:
Antisocials are the ultimate predators. They'll steal your wallet and then blame you for being careless. It's estimated that fifty percent of the people in jail are antisocials (they're the ones that got caught).

The antisocial personality is sometimes referred to as a psychopath or sociopath, although these terms are usually reserved for criminals. The hallmark of the antisocial personality is a pervasive disregard for, and the violation of, the rights of others, and their behavior is usually not modified by negative consequences.

Personality Criteria

The antisocial personality pattern must occur by age 15 years and includes three of the following features from *The Diagnostic and Statistical Manual of Mental Disorders*:

- Failure to conform to social norms with respect to lawful behaviors as indicated by repeatedly performing acts that are the grounds for arrest

- Deceitfulness as indicated by repeated lying, use of aliases, or conning others for personal profit or pleasure

- Impulsivity or failure to plan ahead

- Irritability and aggressiveness as indicated by repeated physical fights or assaults

- Reckless disregard for the safety of self or others

- Consistent irresponsibility, as indicated by three or more of the following:

  A. A pervasive pattern of disregard for and violation of the rights of others by repeated failure to sustain consistent work behavior or honor financial obligations

B. The individual is at least 18 years of age

C. There is evidence of conduct disorder with onset before 15 years of age (delinquent as an adolescent)

D. The occurrence of antisocial behavior is not caused by mental disorders exclusively during the course of schizophrenia or a manic episode

• Lack of remorse, as indicated by being indifferent to or rationalizing having hurt, mistreated, or stolen from another

Social Predators

Studies show that sociopaths account for 20% of the U.S. prison population and between 33-80% of the population of chronic criminal offenders. Although they may have a veneer of sociability, they do not posses sincere social emotions such as love, shame, guilt, empathy or remorse. Benjamin Wolman, who wrote *Antisocial Behavior: Personality Disorders from Hostility to Homicide,* calls them "social predators who selfishly take what they want and do what they please."

Dr. Martha Stout, a Harvard Medical School psychiatrist who wrote *Sociopath Next Door: The Ruthless Versus the Rest of Us*, says that 4% of the population exhibit at least three of the characteristics that distinguish sociopaths: deceitfulness, impulsivity and lack of remorse. She says a chief trait is their charisma. They're often more spontaneous, intense, complex or even sexier than everyone else.

Borderline (or Borderline Traits)

Note:
Experts estimate that a border-line personality disorder has an arrested emotional development level that is equivalent to a two year-old—or even younger (nar-cissists are a little bit older).

People with borderline personality disorders have a pervasive pattern of unstable and intense interpersonal relationships, self-perception and moods.

Personality Criteria

A borderline personality exhibits a pervasive pattern of interpersonal relationships, self-image and affects, and marked impulsivity beginning by early childhood and present in a variety of contexts, as indicated by five (or more) of the following features from *The Diagnostic and Statistical Manual of Mental Disorders*:

- Frantic efforts to avoid real or imagined abandonment

- A pattern of unstable and intense interpersonal relationships characterized by alternating between extremes of idealization and devaluation

- Identity disturbance markedly and persistently unstable self-image or sense of self

- Impulsivity in at least two areas that are potentially self damaging (e.g. spending, sex, substance abuse, reckless driving, binge eating)

- Recurrent suicidal behavior, gestures, or threats, or self-mutilating behavior

- Affective instability due to marked reactivity of mood (e.g. abrupt feelings of extreme negativity usually lasting a few hours and only rarely more than a few days)

- Chronic feelings of emptiness

Quote: "A borderline personality disorder will put suction cups on your soul and suck you dry."

- Unknown

- Inappropriate, intense anger or difficulty controlling anger (e.g. frequent displays of temper, constant anger, recurrent physical fights)

- Transient stress-related paranoid ideas or severe disassociative symptoms

> The best way to deal with personality disordered persons is to not have a relationship with them. But, if you have to have one (i.e. family, boss) you need to limit your interaction and detach any emotional dependence or reliance on that person.

Meet Joel

For those who have a narcissist in their lives, it is important to understand that people with personality disorders do not have a capacity to change. Narcissistic traits, like the traits of other personality disorders, are pervasive.

It's rare that narcissists will seek counseling. Typically, it's the people around them who seek help. Narcissists form relationships with people who are codependent because codependents typically give and give and give with the feeling that their efforts will help the narcissist "change." When I counsel a codependent relative or partner, I try to help them understand that a person with a personality disorder is not "like us." My client Jane is an example of someone who is involved with a narcissist. Her boyfriend Joel's traits are classic.

Jane was referred to me by her family doctor, who felt Jane had stress-related health problems that needed to be evaluated. She had frequent headaches, sleeplessness and low thyroid function that is frequently caused by stress. Jane had confided in her doctor and said that she thought her physical problems might be caused by the problems in her personal relationship. When she came to see me, I asked her to describe her relationship with Joel.

"I've been with Joel for over four years. We just moved in together a year and a half ago. I thought living together and helping him out financially would make things better, but it's been a nightmare and getting worse. He never, ever has thought of me first. He always thinks of himself. He didn't even buy me a birthday present this year.

Quote: "A borderline personality disorder has two categories for others: god or pond scum."

- Guy Shilts

Because personality disorders are pervasive, I asked Jane to describe Joel's relationship with other people in his life starting with his parents.

> "He's rude to both of his parents. When we spend time with them, he rarely asks them what is happening in their life. When we're alone, he talks about them as though they were his worst enemies. I don't see any love in that relationship."

People with personality disorders have traits that are pervasive, and this is the hardest point for the rest of us to understand. It means that they treat everyone the same. Because this is so difficult to comprehend, it is worth repeating over and over to yourself. People with a personality disorder are not like us. They have a dark and scary core. Next, I asked Jane if Joel had close friends.

> "He has one friend named Bob and he's a saint. Joel is always calling him and asking him to do favors for him and Joel never seems to pay him back."

Without realizing it, Jane was describing behavior that sounded pervasive. We moved on to Joel's job and I asked Jane to describe his situation at work.

> "He recently lost his job and blamed it on a bad boss (again). He also said it was my fault because I didn't support him enough or believe in him enough."

Narcissists are predators who are often charming. Their charisma draws people to them. They are often good-looking and very smart. I asked Jane to describe what attracted her to Joel.

> "Joel is very attractive and he knows it. When we met, I was concerned that he would be conceited about his looks but that thought seemed to drift from my mind when he started pursuing me."

I asked Jane if she thought Joel would change.

> "I hope he changes. He was nice to me at one time. Unfortunately, he's only nice when I'm doing what he wants me to do. Otherwise, he gets mad, mean, and puts me down."

For Jane to stay in a relationship with a predator (for more than a day), she has to be extremely codependent. As we've described in previous chapters, codependency is the loss of a sense of self. To understand Jane's feelings or perception about herself, I asked her about her parents.

> "Dad drank up until I was about 14, and you know, he was very self-centered when he was drinking. We almost lost our house at one point. Mom kicked him out, he almost got fired, and I guess he hit bottom then. He's been sober for 15 years now. He still goes to AA and mom still goes to

FYI: We usually don't see people with destructive personality disorders unless they are:

- driving a codependent crazy
- ordered to seek counseling by the court

Al-Anon. Mom put up with all that shit for so long. I used to get so scared and angry at her and him, and now I know she taught me too well how to take care of someone, and that's not a good thing. I also learned that men are selfish, but that they can change, cause my dad did."

Codependents usually have a history of dysfunctional relationships. I asked Jane about her relationships with other men.

"Yeah—I've always taken care of guys. They've always been dopers or drunks. I seem to be a magnet for men with problems."

Jane's Detective Work

Note:
Jane needs to get stronger and redefine her reality. She needs to build up her strengths and minimize her weaknesses.

It's pretty clear that Jane's boyfriend Joel is a narcissist, but I wanted Jane to figure this out for herself. I asked her to fill out a questionnaire and use a notebook to record the details of her personal interactions with Joel. We planned to talk over the answers and compare them to the criteria that the American Psychiatric Association uses to define a narcissist.

Understanding The Narcissist Personality

Personality disorders take advantage of their significant other's weaknesses and they chip away at their strengths. This is what they do and they're very good at it. Readers can use the questions as a guide to help understand the narcissist personality and to help analyze if you're in a relationship with someone who is a narcissist.

Questionnaire

The following questions may be used to evaluate a person in your life who you suspect is a narcissist. Read each question and think about it carefully. Remember that the characteristics in a narcissist's personality are pervasive. In other words, narcissists do not change or have good days and bad days. They treat everyone the same. Because I can't be there in person to help you evaluate your answers, I've included hints that will help you review your responses.

Q: How would you describe [name here] perception of himself or herself?

Hint: Narcissists have a grandiose view of their self-importance.

FYI: Gilderoy Lockhart from the *Harry Potter* novels is a narcissist.

Q: Does [name here] take responsibility for his/her actions?

Hint: People with this personality disorder never take responsibility for their own actions. They blame others.

Q: Does [name here] care about missed appointments or using another person's time?

Hint: A narcissist will take advantage of others around them (they do this to everyone). They have unreasonable expectations and feel that they are "special" and should be treated differently than everyone else.

Q: Does [name here] spend time talking (or bragging) about what he/she intends to accomplish?

Hint: A narcissist is preoccupied with fantasies about their success, power, brilliance, beauty or ideal love. Although they spend enormous amounts of time planning their "schemes," they seldom follow through.

Q: Does [name here] ever apologize for his/her actions?

Hint: A narcissist's sense of entitlement and unreasonable expectations of others means that they will rarely apologize for something that they did or said. Their lack of empathy and their inability to identify with the needs of others will make them oblivious to other people's feelings.

Q: If you took a vacation or a day trip with [name here] and you took a camera along, would [name here] want to take pictures of you?

FYI: Livia Soprano, from the HBO series *The Sopranos*, is a narcissist. She's the family matriarch who is scheming, manipulative, conniving and abusive.

Hint: Narcissists often want to associate with special or high-status people (or institutions) and may not value photographs of friends or relatives.

Q: When you feel it's your time to tell [name here] about the events in your life, does he/she:
  a) Change the subject?
  b) Look at his/her watch?
  c) Show signs of being distracted?

Hint: The narcissist's requirement of excessive admiration means that they will not be interested in events that take place in other people's lives. Although they may have manners and display a superficial amount of interest, it will be easy to see their lack of genuine interest.

Q: How do you feel after spending time with [name here]?

Hint: A narcissist will drain you. You will be depleted of energy because of their need for uninterrupted empathy.

Psychological Weight Training

Note:
Once a person understands that people with personality disorders are different, the next step is to develop coping strategies to protect themselves.

People with a weak sense of self will have a hard time identifying a narcissist, and they often have a hard time breaking free. Although Joel's narcissism was a destructive influence in their relationship, Jane's "sense of self" was also a problem. Jane could break up with Joel but unless she strengthened her self-esteem, she would most likely attract a similar predator.

If you're in a relationship with a person who has a personality disorder, it is critically important that you build up your strengths and minimize your weaknesses. Keep in mind that you have a far greater ability to change than your personality-disordered loved one. Consider the following strategies:

Keep Interactions to a Minimum

This strategy may be difficult but it is the most effective. Avoiding a personality-disordered person and insulating yourself with space is a very healthy option. If you're having trouble with this option, ask yourself this question:

> "Has the personality-disordered person in your life ever shown signs that he/she has changed?"

Note: Review Rule #12: The Best Predictor of Future Behavior is Past Behavior Unless the Person Works Very Hard to Change.

Detach Emotionally

Previously, we have talked about electromagnetic positive and negative charges associated with positive and negative emotional states. Your mental health requires that you learn to move your Emotional Valence Value (EVV) to a

FYI: In psychoanalysis, the narcissistic personality disorder is known as megalomania.

neutral value of zero or to some positive value. Here are some techniques that may help:

See Yourself As a Temporary Visitor

One of the keys to detaching from a person or situation is to see the scene as temporary—as though you are only a visitor. If necessary, think of yourself as an observer and the people involved as characters in a play. Imagine:

• your personality disordered loved one as a fictitious character in a drama

• his/her behavior is of no consequence to you

• as an audience member, your emotions are either neutral or positive

Ignore Attacks and/or Criticisms

In order to successfully detach emotionally, it's important that you do not react to your personality-disordered loved one's attacks or criticisms. To maintain your emotional valence at zero or at some positive value, you'll need to make sure you do not respond to his/her need to:

• feel superior

• criticize you

• blackmail you

• manipulate you

• make you feel guilty

Ask Yourself: "What Would Guy Do?"

As your psychological weight trainer, I can confidently say that the following strategies are suitable for any encounters with personality-disordered people:

FYI: The narcissistic personality disorder occurs more frequently in men than in women.

Rebel

Remember the rebel in chapter one? People who are abused by personality-disordered people often have low self-esteem and they need to rebel. The most effective way to rebel is to quietly disappear and not do what the personality-disordered person wants you to do.

Do the Opposite

A quiet disappearing act is a passive form of resistance when a personality-disordered person tries to control or manipulate you. A more confrontational approach is to do the exact opposite of what they're trying to get you to do.

If he/she...	Confrontational Opposite
Insists on eating at only one restaurant...	Make a reservation elsewhere.
Threatens to not show up for a gathering if you invite someone he/she doesn't like.	Invite the person anyway.

Be forewarned that the personality-disordered person will need to be in control and will probably go his/her separate way.

Warning: If your personality-disordered person is violent, you cannot rebel or confront him/her. You will need to be clever and sneak away. Susan Murphy-Milano's *Moving Out, Moving On* is an excellent workbook for learning how to end a destructive relationship.

Quote: "Pathological narcissism can be induced in adulthood by celebrity, wealth, and fame."

- Dr. Robert Millman
  Professor of Psychiatry
  New York Hospital

Negotiate

Personality-disordered people feel a sense of entitlement, and they may have no problem with manipulation. When you have gained control of your emotions, you may want to try to train him/her to respect your boundaries. Here are some steps:

Step #1 *Determine the Consequences*

Before you even begin negotiations, you will need to decide if you're strong enough to stand your ground should he/she make a decision to ignore your conditions. For example, be prepared to withdraw for a while to make a clear statement about consequences.

Step #2 *Be Clear About Your Boundaries*

When you're ready to negotiate, you will need to be *extra* clear about your expectations. Be sure the personality-disordered person understands the consequences for noncompliance.

Step #3 *Be Resilient to Emotional Triggers*

Expect the personality-disordered person to try to manipulate you emotionally. It's likely that they have many years of practice at pushing your buttons and you will need to be strong.

Engaging in negotiations with a personality-disordered person will not be easy, especially if you're in a relationship with them. Be ready to implement consequences if you see that the negotiations are not working.

Alcoholism and Drug Addiction Can Look a Lot Like Narcissism

Substance abuse is an expression that describes an addiction to alcohol and/or drugs, and a person who is dependent on either one of these has behavior patterns that can look like every major psychiatric disorder.

Addiction is Toxic to a Relationship

I've added substance abuse to this chapter because it's toxic to any relationship, and an addict can look a lot like a narcissist:

- They're self-centered
- They lie
- They may steal for their drugs or alcohol
- They often have severe mood swings

Lies About Drugs or Alcohol

If an addict lies about his/her alcohol or drug use, it may be hard to determine the source of their problem. Twenty years ago, I counseled a man who said he put a gun to his head but didn't pull the trigger. On the surface, his condition looked like depression anxiety disorder. However, when I asked him about his drug usage, he finally owned up and said he felt the most depressed after an eight ball (*or a lot of cocaine*).

Quote: "The time is always right to do what is right."

- Martin Luther King, Jr.

"I know he cheated on me because he doesn't have a conscience. I shot him because I don't either."

CONCLUSION

Mental Health Is A Quest For Enlightenment

Finally, in conclusion, let me say just this.

- Peter Sellers

"*We've covered a lot of material in these thirteen chapters and it may be overwhelming at first. It might be helpful to re-read the rules that are most pertinent to you, reflect on them and take the steps necessary for positive change. My hope is that the book will help you move from fear-based to love-based relationships; move from denial to self-understanding; to live in the present while you reflect on the past and plan for the future; and to realize that we're all in this together and are part of a greater whole. Your quest to face your own truths or to get beyond your denial won't be easy but can definitely lead you to a happier and more fulfilling life.*

I wish you well on your journey!"

For more information or consulting requests send an e-mail to gshiltscrossroads@charterinternet.net.

Index

Drug-free, 325
DSM-III, 340
DSM-IV, 340
DSM-V, 340
Duality, 282
Duchovny, David, 254
Duke, Patty, 108
Dyer, Wayne, 32, 33, 208, 279
Dynamic, 129, 151, 172
Dysfunction, 13, 42, 43, 44, 50, 54, 55, 58, 59, 61, 64,
    65, 75, 76, 77, 78, 87, 89, 104, 122, 123, 124, 125,
    128, 135, 148, 152, 161, 163, 165, 216, 232, 277,
    298, 300, 310, 315, 316, 317, 354
Dyslexic, 10

E

Earhart, Amelia, 301
Ed, 319, 320, 321, 322
EdD (Educational doctor), 55
Eddie, 78, 79
Edison, Thomas,s 290
Effective communication, 227, 228
Effectiveness Training for Women, 247
800-THE LOST, 74
Einstein, Albert, 107, 199
Elephant in the middle of the room, 308
Elevated blood pressure, 267
Embed memories, 128
Emily, 129, 146
Emotional abuse, 95
Emotional catharsis, 76
Emotional centers, 294
Emotional connections, 97, 101, 105
Emotional dependence, 350
Emotional deprivation, 97
Emotional development, 76, 349
Emotional imprinting, 127
Emotional memories, 294
Emotional scaling tool, 127
Emotional stability, 50
Emotional trauma, 51
Emotional triggers, 34, 128, 361

Emotional valence value (EVV), 358
Emotionally distant, 95, 315
Emotionally immature, 147
Emotionally neglectful, 217
Emotions, 38, 39, 40, 42, 72, 75, 90, 125, 131, 132,
    145, 156, 192, 230, 233, 234, 238, 243, 282, 294,
    310, 316, 348, 359, 361
Empathetic, 161
Empathy, 141, 191, 339, 344, 345, 346, 348,
    356, 357
Empire Strikes Back, The, 299
Employee Assistance Program, General Motors, 105
Enabler, 44, 46, 60, 69, 124, 161, 163
Endorphins, 294
ENFJ, 175, 196, 198, 200, 201, 202
ENFP, 175, 183, 194, 198, 200, 202
England, 228
Enmeshed, 125, 269, 277
Enteric (gut) system, 294
Entitlement, 345, 356, 361
ENTJ, 175, 195, 198, 200
ENTP, 175, 194, 198, 200
Environment, 13. 32, 48, 78, 94, 151, 194, 266
Ephron, Nora, 337
Epinephrine, 294
EQ for Everybody, 232
Equilibrium, 43, 53, 282
Escaping, 64
*Etiquette in Society, in Business, in
    Politics and at Home*, 257
Evans, Linda, 207
Evans-Wentz, Walter, 166
Evolution, 32, 45
Excel, 45, 61, 100
Exploitation, 108
Exploring patterns, 177
Explosive temper, 240
Extinction burst, 334
Extreme codependency, 161
Extreme dependence, 156
Extrovert (E), 138, 139, 169, 174, 175, 177, 181, 183,
    184, 185, 187, 188, 189, 190, 194, 195, 196, 197,
    200, 201, 202, 203, 206, 220, 222

CPSIA information can be obtained at www.ICGtesting.com
Printed in the USA
240396LV00002B/5/A